Bakke's SHAKESPEARE

ROMEO & JULIET

Theran Press

Theran Press is the academic imprint of Silver Goat Media.

Theran is dedicated to authentic partnerships with our academic associates, to the quality design of scholarly books, and to elite standards of peer review.

Theran seeks to free intellectuals from the confines of traditional publishing.

Theran scholars are authorities and revolutionaries in their respective fields.

Theran encourages new models for generating and distributing knowledge.

For our creatives, for our communities, for our world.

WWW.THERANPRESS.ORG

BAKKE'S SHAKESPEARE: ROMEO AND JULIET.

Published by Silver Goat Media, LLC, Fargo, ND 58108. This publication is protected by copyright, and permission should be obtained from the publisher prior to any reproduction, storage in a retrieval system, or transmission in any form or by any means, electronic, mechanical, photocopying, recording, or likewise. SGM books are available at discounts, regardless of quantity, for K-12 schools, non-profits, or other educational institutions. To obtain permission(s) to use material from this work, or to order in bulk, please submit a written request to Silver Goat Media, LLC, PO Box 2336 Fargo, ND 58108, or contact SGM directly at: info@silvergoatmedia.com.

 This book was designed and produced by Silver Goat Media, LLC. Fargo, ND U.S.A. www.silvergoatmedia.com SGM, the SGM goat, Theran Press, and the Theran theta are trademarks of Silver Goat Media, LLC.

Edited by Cady Rutter © 2023 SGM
Cover design & typeset by Jonathan Rutter © 2023 SGM
Cover illustration (digitally modified detail): ART File S528r1 no.132 part 10, image 29304, Folger Shakespeare Library.

ISBN-13: 978-1-944296-23-0

 A portion of the annual proceeds from the sale of this book is donated to The Rourke Art Gallery + Museum www.therourke.org

Bakke's SHAKESPEARE

ROMEO & JULIET

Translated by

ANTHONY BAKKE

THERAN PRESS

What actual students are saying about Bakke's Shakespeare: ROMEO AND JULIET

"I liked how it made the play seem less overwhelming and helped break down the language to make it simpler to understand. It also helped when I went back to the original text after reading the Bakke version because it was easier to understand the language once I understood the basic plot line."

"I think it helped me understand the play of *Romeo and Juliet* a lot better in modern English. It is an effective tool for teaching kids how to decode Shakespearean English."

"I liked that it was very engaging and fun. I was able to understand the play. We were also able to complete full acts in a single day. And I would feel that it was easier to understand because it's more of a teen's perspective."

"I loved how it modernized the play and made it a lot more comedic. It pokes fun at the drama and hysteria that Shakespeare had written and makes a lot of the awkward moments of Shakespeare funny and easier to read. It really breaks the fourth wall and puts the harder-to-read sentences in better-to-understand modernized language."

"It really helped me understand what was happening in the play. It also made the humor make more sense, so I thought it was funnier."

"It was more fun and helped to keep the class going. There was nothing that didn't work well with the Bakke version."

"It takes the Shakespearean language and turns it into an understandable, modern transcript without taking out any of the details. The Bakke version takes incomprehensible words and turns them into easy-to-read, funny, useful sentences. It doesn't leave anything out or stray from Shakespeare's tone. It makes reading the play much more enjoyable as well as educational. I very much recommend this version of *Romeo and Juliet* to both students and teachers learning about *Romeo and Juliet* and its difficult language."

"Imma be honest, the Bakke version saved my grade in this class. I would HIGHLY recommend it for classes in the future."

"I really liked the Bakke version because it made the old jokes make more sense, it made the acting more fun, it made complex words and phrases a lot easier, and it made really long speeches into two sentences. I liked that it kept some words and ways of talking while still making sense. Finally, it kept the students super engaged because they knew they'd still understand what's going on while getting to have fun."

"I liked the Bakke version of *Romeo and Juliet* because it helped the class act out the play, which was a big part of how I understood the play. I participated—or wanted to participate more—when I knew we would be reading Bakke's version."

"I think it's very good because I understood it more. More students engage with the Bakke version. It kept me awake. It's good for students who were really confused, like me."

"I liked that the Bakke version of *Romeo and Juliet* made it easily understandable. Shakespeare is pretty difficult to understand so the Bakke version really helped me make sense of the story."

"I loved it! It was so funny, and I remember myself and my classmates looking forward to reading it all week long. It was just fun. Don't know how to explain it other than it was super funny but still true to the play."

"The Bakke version took the original comedy of *Romeo and Juliet* and brought it into modern times. It made the whole unit a lot less serious and way more fun."

What actual teachers are saying about
Bakke's Shakespeare: ROMEO AND JULIET

Anthony Bakke has created a work of both erudition and entertainment! He has captured the essence of the Bard, both his humor and depth, in a translation of Shakespeare's work that will appeal to all audiences! My ninth graders loved every word! They laughed. They cried. They learned!

—ROBERT MAAS, *Maple Grove High School, Maple Grove, MN*

The best compliment a teacher can receive is a student asking, "Can we do that again tomorrow?" When I first gave my ninth graders a copy of Mr. Bakke's translation of Shakespeare's *Romeo and Juliet*, I watched as students read aloud and unfurled with laughter, joy— and comprehension. The next day, three boys rushed up to my desk to ask, "Are we reading the Bakke version again today?" For a writer or teacher, no greater appraisal exists. I am thrilled this project exists. It will reach and engage countless students. If you believe in the power of literature, equity, and engagement—this is your resource.

—ABBI DION, *Robbinsdale Armstrong High School, Plymouth, MN*

Bakke's Shakespeare has been pivotal in engaging students in my classes because it uses modern language, humor, and slang. The text is entirely in keeping with the core of *Romeo and Juliet*, but it's so much more accessible. I would recommend it to any teacher who cares about literacy in a world in which fewer students come to school with a love of reading. *Bakke's Shakespeare* takes a creative approach that students are sure to love!

—KAIA HIRT, *Champlin Park High School, Champlin, MN*

I used *Bakke's Shakespeare* with my ninth-grade English classes. They found it hilarious and enjoyable—there was a lot of laughter!

—KIRSTEN BIGHIA, *Robbinsdale Armstrong High School, Plymouth, MN*

Sometimes when old meets new, it's a recipe for disaster; this is not the case for *Bakke's Shakespeare: Romeo and Juliet.* Anthony Bakke's contemporary take on one of Shakespeare's most iconic plays is the perfect supplemental text for teaching *Romeo and Juliet.* I've used this in my ninth-grade classes for three years now, and each time I've had similar results: students are more engaged and actually seem to enjoy the reading, which is what we hope for as teachers. I recommend using this, 100%.

—LINNEA HALEY, *Robbinsdale Armstrong High School, Plymouth, MN*

My favorite quote while using *Bakke's Shakespeare* was something along the lines of, "Shakespeare needs to write his books like that!" It is literally my Shakespeare/*Romeo and Juliet* bible. I can't imagine teaching the unit without it. It aids in comprehension, but also decodes complex text. And what I love most about it is that it truly reaches every student regardless of ability or attitude. It makes students excited to read Shakespeare because they know they get to read this version too.

—BRITTNI PARRISH, *Eden Valley-Watkins High School, Eden Valley, MN*

This book is dedicated to my wife, Kirsten, who always believes in me, and to my daughter, MacKenna, who always inspires me.

CONTENTS

INTRODUCTION

I love Shakespeare. His plays and poetry are still considered the absolute pinnacle of the English language. His stories have been performed the world over. Whether it be Elizabeth Taylor, Marlon Brando, and Charlton Heston; or Kenneth Branagh, Patrick Stewart, Anthony Hopkins, and Ian McKellen; or Mel Gibson, Leonardo DiCaprio, Keanu Reeves, Denzel Washington, Orlando Bloom, and Russell Brand, every actor considers it an honor and a privilege to play one of Shakespeare's great heroes or heroines and will always jump at the chance to play one. The characters in Shakespeare's plays are complicated and nuanced. They span the emotional spectrum and force actors to challenge themselves to be at their acting best. And what actor worth anything wouldn't want to have their name attached to characters like Hamlet, Macbeth, King Lear, Othello, Romeo, and Juliet? Because of the demand for these plays, it seems like every year we get a new movie or TV show dedicated to one of Shakespeare's plays. And why not? They are not only filled with iconic characters but also with universal themes that resonate within our lives no matter what age we live in. They cover virtually every interest! Whether your interests lie in politics, love, romance, violence, corruption, family drama, cross-dressing, history, war, trickery, or anything in between, there is a Shakespeare play for that. His plays have stood the test of time and are as popular now, centuries after they were written, as any other era since William Shakespeare put ink to paper. There is simply no one else who comes close.

As a high school English teacher for nearly two decades, and an English major in the years prior to that, I have grown a great love and respect for the Bard of Avon as I have taught works such as *Romeo and Juliet*, *Macbeth*, *Julius Caesar*, *Hamlet*, and *A Midsummer Night's Dream* every year of my career. And based on the start to this introduction, you would think that every student who graces my classroom would be tingling with anticipation and excitement to read these literary masterpieces! But the truth is, that is not the case. Whenever a new school year starts and I give a preview of the year to come and mention that we will be reading a Shakespearean play, there is an audible groan and an almost tangible feeling of dread and gloom. Eyes roll. How is this possible? Teens have historically loved modernized versions of Shakespeare's plays, such as *West Side Story (Romeo and Juliet)*, *10 Things I Hate About You (The Taming of the Shrew)*, *She's the Man (12th Night)*, or *O (Othello)*. The themes and characterizations of Macbeth can be found in the movie *Scarface* as well as in the TV show *Breaking Bad*. Heck, whether it was intentional or not, *The Lion King* was basically *Hamlet* and it is one of the most successful animated movies of all time! So the problem does not lie in the plots or characters. The problem lies in the language. And it was that understanding that led me to this: the "Bakke's Shakespeare" version of *Romeo and Juliet*.

I want to reiterate that I love the language of Shakespeare. The issue is that teenagers typically don't. At least not right away. They don't like things they don't understand—especially when they are expected to comprehend them and are being tested on them. They get frustrated. And every English teacher everywhere is asked the same questions: "Why can't they just speak normal?" "Why do they talk like this?" The most common response to this is, "Well, that's just the way they talked back then!" Umm . . . sorta. Of course, the English language has evolved over the last four hundred years. It would be naive to think that four hundred years from now, the English language will be the exact same as it is now. But this is an overly simplistic answer. I don't know about you, but my everyday conversation does not consist of monologues in iambic pentameter. I don't usually speak in rhyme when I am very emotional; and when I encounter a pretty girl, I am not loquacious enough to create a sonnet on the spot to convey my love. Further, I guarantee the people of Shakespeare's time did not either. To really understand why Shakespeare wrote the way he did, we must go back to the purpose of language in different periods of time. The goal of language has changed over the years. In today's society, we want to get to the point. Don't beat around the bush. Keep it simple. In fact, if you can convey your idea in 140 characters or less, all the better. We are an instant gratification society, and our use of language reflects that. In Shakespeare's time, the goal of language was the direct opposite: Why be simple when you can be poetic? Why say something anybody can say when you can say something in a way that has never been heard before? And if you can include a rhetorical device or classical allusion, even better. Why say "it's dawn" when you can say "the gray-eyed morn smiles on the frowning night, / Check'ring the Eastern clouds with streaks of light" (*Romeo and Juliet* 2.3.1-2), or " . . . envious streaks / Do lace the severing clouds in yonder east" (*Romeo and Juliet* 3.5.7-8).[1] Why say "I won't cry" when you can say "and let not women's weapons, water drops, stain my man's cheeks" (*King Lear* 2.4.273–274). Why say "should I kill myself?" when you can say "to be or not to be, that is the question" (*Hamlet* 3.1.55). Shakespeare's goal was to bring the English language to new heights and to take our language and make it poetry. It was also what people expected and wanted. If they were going to pay the price of admission, they didn't want to hear everyday language. They could hear that in the marketplace! They wanted to hear the English language at its finest. Once all of this is explained, students have a stronger understanding as to why Shakespeare is beautiful but exceedingly difficult to follow. And unfortunately, understanding why Shakespeare wrote the way he did does not help students understand the language any faster. So while they understand the why, they still don't want to read it.

As their teacher, it is my job to get them to read, comprehend, analyze, and—hopefully—enjoy Shakespeare. I've tried different approaches, but we always read the play in class. I never ask my students to go home and read Shakespeare by themselves with the expectation that they understand it. When I was an English major taking a course called "Shakespeare" at St. Cloud State University, I struggled with that. How can I expect high school students to do it? So we read in class. The problem with this is that it takes so long to do it. In the early stages, I am stopping after nearly every line, either translating it or asking the students if they can make sense of it. It can be cumbersome and frustrating as some kids start to get it and others are still lost. It would take an entire quarter of the school year to finish the unit. Eventually, several years ago, my colleagues and I were redesigning the ninth-grade English course, and we discussed how we could do this unit better. What we decided is that we could still study the language and work on comprehension of this complex text without reading the entire play. We could focus on the major scenes, read them in class, and then really spend time decoding and analyzing the language. We read act 1, scene 5 (when Romeo and Juliet first meet), act 2, scene 2 (the balcony scene), act 3, scene 1 (the deaths of Tybalt and Mercutio), and act 5, scene 3 (the final scene) completely in the original Shakespearean text. These are lengthy, crucial scenes where major plot advancements are made; we delve into the Shakespearean language and spend at least a couple of days on each of them. For the rest of the play, we had the freedom to convey plot points in other ways in order to keep the story line coherent while also being more efficient with our time. We used video clips, graphic novels, and summaries.

---

[1]   Quoted lines are referenced from the Folger Shakespeare Library editions of Shakespeare's plays.

While this was much better for time, the problem I came to was losing the interactive elements of the unit that I loved so much. I firmly believe that Shakespeare was meant to be seen and heard, not just read. So when we read the entirety of the play in class, I would have students volunteer for roles, come up to the front of the class and stage the scenes, and have some fun. Now, other than the few scenes we chose to read in the original Shakespeare, it was mostly seatwork and individual activities. I wanted to get that interactivity and play immersion back. I thought maybe we could still do some kind of performance with some modern translations. So I looked around and explored different versions. Unfortunately, I didn't like what I found. The translations were dull and dry. They didn't convey the humor and passion that Shakespeare did. I wanted the students to be engaged and have fun, and I didn't see that happening with the materials that were out there.

I decided I could do better.

I sat down and wrote a new version of the first few scenes that was not a perfect translation but still stayed true to the heart of the story. I wrote the characters with fidelity to Shakespeare's portrayal. I modernized the language while keeping the humor of these scenes intact. I imagined that if Shakespeare were writing today, knowing how we like our language straight to the point while incorporating an abundance of tongue-in-cheek humor and sarcasm, that he would write the play somewhat like this. I did my best to follow the plot and dialogue as Shakespeare wrote it, but make it fun to read (i.e., not a direct, pure translation). I tried it in my classes with act 1, scenes 1–4. We got through these scenes (which are, essentially, just the exposition of the play) in one day; in the past, it would have taken a week. More importantly, the kids loved it. And most importantly, they understood it. We were able to move into act 1, scene 5 with the kids engaged in the story, invested in the characters, and ready to find out what happened next. Later on, I did a couple of scenes in act 3 to bridge the gap between act 3, scenes 1 and 5. And again, it was a hit. They understood it and started asking for it in the following scenes. I gave it to my colleagues in case they wanted to give it a shot. A number of them used it and came back to tell me that their students absolutely loved it and were raving about it. I started getting stopped in the hallways by students asking if I was Mr. Bakke. When I said yes, they told me they loved the Bakke version. We used this for a couple of years and these scenes seemed to be the highlight of the unit. I decided that if it was this effective in engaging the students and helping them not only understand the text but actually enjoy the story, then a Bakke version of the entire play could become a wonderful teaching tool. And over the last number of years, that is what I did.

I want to be clear that I don't want people to see this as a replacement for reading Shakespeare. The beauty of the man's work is in his language. I can't duplicate what he did. We still read select scenes of their original text and study them thoroughly. I do want readers to see this version as a means of furthering understanding and igniting a spark of interest and engagement in those students who might otherwise shut down or quit, not believing they could ever "get it." I've told my students that I don't mind when they use websites like Sparknotes.com, or things like CliffsNotes, so long as they use them as supplements to the actual text to help them understand things that they would not be able to get on their own. It is with this idea that I started adding in my own thoughts and analysis to certain scenes and characters. These are often talking points from my classes that I thought would add even more understanding of the text and open the door for discussion—and even some personal relevance. I've set this commentary apart in footnotes so it is clear when the thoughts, analysis, and opinions are mine, and mine alone. I truly believe that this can be an invaluable tool that teachers everywhere can use to engage their students in Shakespeare so that those eye rolls and groans can be replaced with genuine excitement. Outside the classroom, anyone can pick this version up and have a fun reading experience on their own. I think it is a fun read no matter who you are; I did my best to make it so. And maybe . . . just maybe . . . after reading this, fully confident in your knowledge of the plot, you may be interested in reading the entire play as Shakespeare wrote it. That would be the ultimate reward!

So I now invite you to read the "Bakke's Shakespeare" version of *Romeo and Juliet* and, hopefully, ignite or reignite your love of Shakespeare, get inspired to go back to that original text, and see that a funny, exciting, heart-wrenching tragic tale can be told in multiple ways: (1) a quasitranslation with an emphasis on storytelling, and (2) well . . . Shakespeare!

Enjoy!

—Anthony Bakke

CAST OF CHARACTERS

THE MONTAGUES

ROMEO: Romeo Montague is the leading male in the play. You probably guessed that based on the title. He is often depicted and remembered as the ideal romantic lead in the greatest love story ever told. The truth is, as Shakespeare wrote him, he is an incredibly immature, desperate, impulsive, passionate, overemotional, highly dramatic, hopeless romantic teenager who lets his emotions and feelings run his life rather than utilizing any semblance of logic or reason. He loves the idea of love, with a focus on physical beauty. When he is not focused on love (or lust as the case may be), he is a very witty, fun-loving young man who others seem to legitimately like, care about, and respect. He is also apparently pretty good with a sword.

LORD MONTAGUE: Romeo's father and the patriarch of the Montague family and, along with Lord Capulet, one of the men who holds the grudge that has fueled a feud between the two families for years. He cares deeply about his son, Romeo, and will defend him when needed.

LADY MONTAGUE: Romeo's mother and the matriarch of the Montague family. She only speaks in act 1, scene 1. In the entire play, she is only on stage at the end of act 3, scene 1. So other than her concern for Romeo, there really isn't much to say about her.

BENVOLIO: Romeo's cousin and one of his closest friends. He supports and tries to cheer up his cousin when needed. He gives good advice and knows Romeo well. According to Mercutio, he is a willing fighter who will throw down when he can. He is also extremely honest, as evidenced by the fact that whenever something happens, he is the first one people ask to explain the situation.

ABRAM: A Montague servant; he only exists to exemplify the intensity of the feud between the Montague and Capulet families. He is involved in the brawl that opens the play, shown defending the Montague name against some Capulets who were insulting him and his master. He is not seen or heard from for the rest of the play.

BALTHASAR: Romeo's servant. He is trustworthy and honest and fulfills his duties well . . . sometimes almost too well. You will see what I mean in the final act!

THE CAPULETS

JULIET: Juliet Capulet is the leading lady of the play. I'm sure you knew that. She is a thirteen-year-old girl that has not entertained the idea of love and marriage until meeting Romeo. She shows flashes of rationality but also shows an abundance of impulsivity, passion, desperation, and an "all-or-nothing" attitude. She deals in absolutes with very little nuance. She is also apparently very beautiful as she has two men vying for her hand.

LORD CAPULET: Juliet's father and the patriarch of the Capulet family and, along with Lord Montague, one of the men who holds the grudge that has fueled the feud between the two families for years. Lord Capulet is one of the most complex characters in the play. We see several different sides of his personality—from respectful, jovial, understanding, and loving to passionate, insulting, abusive, and violent. He cares deeply about two things: his daughter and his reputation. And sometimes those two things incite conflict.

LADY CAPULET: Juliet's mother and the matriarch of the Capulet family; she is a typical aristocratic wife and mother from this era. She is far younger than her husband (she is roughly twenty-six, whereas he is probably around fifty) and does not seem to be especially close to her daughter (she can't remember her own daughter's age!). She cares for Juliet deeply but is not especially involved in the raising of the child. She takes her role as lady of the Capulet house seriously and defends the family when needed.

NURSE: The Nurse is Juliet's real motherly influence. She raised Juliet from birth. She is called Nurse because she was a wet nurse to Juliet. This means that she was pregnant and gave birth around the same time as Lady Capulet and was hired to nurse Juliet so that someone as important as Lady Capulet wouldn't be tasked with breastfeeding at all hours. Unfortunately, the Nurse's own child, Susan, died young. It seems that the Nurse treats Juliet as if she were her own child. She is Juliet's closest and most trusted confidante, and her greatest goal is to see Juliet happy. She will do whatever she can to make that happen, even going against Lord and Lady Capulet. She can also be a talkative and annoying source of comic relief.

TYBALT: Juliet's cousin, Tybalt, is a very angry and violent young man. He takes the feud very seriously and will fight whenever the mood strikes him. He is a trained swordsman, and his hatred of all Montagues is one of the instigating factors that leads to the ensuing tragedy.

PETER: Nurse's servant. He is something of an idiot and often used for comic relief.

PETRUCHIO: Tybalt's servant. He barely speaks. There is not much else to say.

SAMPSON AND GREGORY: Two Capulet servants. They serve the same role as Abram of the Montagues. They are used to exemplify the feud between the two families. They open the play discussing their disdain of the Montagues and then instigate the initial brawl by using gestures and words to insult the Montague men. Like Abram, they are not heard from after act 1, scene 1.

CAPULET'S COUSIN: He serves as someone for Lord Capulet to talk to at the party. As far as I can tell, the only thing we know about him is that he and Capulet are close to the same age. They let the audience know that they are no spring chickens . . . meaning they are around fifty or so.

THE ROYAL FAMILY

PRINCE: His full name is Prince Escalus, and he rules Verona. He is strong and sticks with his convictions. He hates the feud between the families and hates how it is tearing the city apart. He does what he can to try and stop it and eventually will succeed . . . but at a very steep personal cost.

PARIS: Count Paris is the cousin of the Prince and seems to be a pretty good guy. He desires to marry Juliet and is the metaphorical "monkey wrench" thrown into the mix which forces the escalation of the drama. He does everything he is supposed to do but is often seen as unlikeable because of his role as Romeo's main romantic rival.

MERCUTIO: The other cousin of the Prince and Romeo's best friend. He is the coolest guy in the play and he loves to make dirty jokes. In truth, he is the type of vulgar guy who will try and make everything into a dirty joke. He is funny, witty, and always an audience favorite. He cares a lot about Romeo and wants to cheer him up when needed. He will also defend him against all enemies, verbally or physically.

PARIS'S PAGE: A servant to Paris; he will follow Paris's instructions even when it forces him to face his fears.

OTHERS

FRIAR LAWRENCE: Friar Lawrence is the resident holy man. He is the trusted confidante of Romeo, the confessor of Juliet, and the preacher of choice for Lord Capulet. He plays a crucial role in bringing Romeo and Juliet together as well as the unfortunate series of events that lead to ultimate tragedy. He is a good man who tries to fix the problems he sees but does not always see the potential consequences of his plans. He is an expert in herbal medicines and potions . . . which may play a role in the play.

FRIAR JOHN: A messenger for Friar Lawrence. All we can really say about him is that he apparently does not like to travel alone.

APOTHECARY: A desperate and impoverished man who is willing to break the law to help improve his life. He specializes in potions and medicines (an apothecary is an old term for a pharmacist).

CITIZENS: The people who live in Verona and who are on stage for crowd scenes. Not much else to say.

MUSICIANS: Kind of self-explanatory. People who play music for special events and parties like, oh I don't know, let's say weddings and funerals.

WATCHMEN: The Watch is the term for the police. First Watch, Second Watch, and Third Watch are the ones who watch over the city of Verona and investigate any crimes. They guard the city at night and are tasked with keeping the citizens safe.

SERVINGMEN: Self-explanatory. They are servants.

CHORUS: The Chorus has nothing to do with music. He is an actual character who, in this play, serves in the role of narrator. He is the only one who speaks directly to the audience providing context, previews, and summary. He delivers both prologues using the poetic structure of a sonnet.[2]

---

2   A sonnet is a type of poem that is fourteen lines long that starts with three quatrains (set of four lines) and ends with a couplet (set of two lines). It employs an abab rhyme structure and is written entirely in iambic pentameter (five sets of stressed and unstressed syllables—meaning each line will be ten syllables long). Shakespeare loved sonnets. He wrote 154 of them. This play has three of them in it: the two choruses and one in act 1, scene 5. See if you can find it!

ROMEO AND JULIET

PROLOGUE [3]

Enter CHORUS.

CHORUS:
Two families of equal social rank
(In Verona where this story takes place),
Rekindle an old feud with a new prank,
Where red blood is shed on a neighbor's face.

But now these two families will produce
Two kids destined to fall in love and die;
Their unfortunate life choices let loose,
End their families' hatred with a cry.

The story of their love and Death's errand
And their parents' hate and continued rage,
Which only their two children's deaths could end,
Will be the two-hour story on this stage.

So if you can watch and pay attention,
You'll get details and the resolution!

---

[3] This and the act 2 prologue are in the form of a sonnet. These are NOT written in the original text but in my own version/translation of it. I decided that I had to keep the sonnet form if I was going to do this justice!

ACT 1

ACT 1, SCENE 1

SAMPSON: I really hate the Montagues. We will not take their insults, and the fact that they are alive is an insult to every Capulet like you and me! If one were here right now . . . oooo I wanna fight them!

GREGORY: But you're a wuss.

SAMPSON: Am not. I wanna kill all the Montague men and take the virginity of the Montague women. I'm man-pretty.

GREGORY: Yeah, except your "member" is a dried-up fish! Hey! Here come some of Montague's men!

SAMPSON: Let's fight them! But let's make them start it. That way, the law is on our side! I'll bite my thumb at them, which is super insulting!

GREGORY: OK!

Sampson bites thumb.

ABRAM: Dude . . . what the heck? Did you really just bite your thumb at us?

SAMPSON: Umm . . . maybe . . . wanna fight?

ABRAM: No.

SAMPSON: I will if you wanna throw down. My boss is as good as yours!

ABRAM: Not any better.

SAMPSON: He's way better!

ABRAM: LIAR!

SAMPSON: Bring it, sucka!

They fight. Enter BENVOLIO *(a Montague, Romeo's cousin).*

BENVOLIO: *(drawing sword)* Stop it! Break it up!

Enter TYBALT *(a Capulet, Juliet's cousin).*

TYBALT *(to* BENVOLIO*):* You're fighting with the servants? Dude . . . turn thee, Benvolio; look upon thy death.

BENVOLIO: Man, I'm trying to break this up! Help me or get outta here!

4

TYBALT: You have your sword out and you talk of peace? I hate the word as I hate Hell, all Montagues, and you. Come on!

They fight. A crowd forms around them like any fight in the school halls. (No cell phone videos though.)

Enter CAPULET *and* LADY CAPULET.

CAPULET: A fight? I want in! Gimme my sword, woman.

LADY CAPULET: Seriously? No. You're old.

Enter MONTAGUE *and* LADY MONTAGUE.

MONTAGUE: A fight with Capulet? I'm so in.

LADY MONTAGUE: Seriously? No. You're old.

Enter PRINCE *and his entourage.*

PRINCE: What the . . . ? Dang it Montague and Capulet. Everybody stop! Throw your weapons down! NOW! This is the third time a fight has broken out because of you two and your stupid feud.[4] This is ridiculous and I've had enough. If anybody is caught fighting again because of this feud, I will execute them. I'm not kidding! You fight, you die. 'Cos violence solves violence. Boom. Drop the mic. Capulet, you're coming with me. Montague, I'll see you later. Once more, on pain of death, all men depart. We out.

Exit all but MONTAGUE, LADY MONTAGUE, *and* BENVOLIO.

MONTAGUE: Benvolio, what happened?

BENVOLIO: Umm. There was a fight and I tried to break it up. Tybalt came and said some mean things, so I fought him.

LADY MONTAGUE: Where's Romeo? I'm glad he wasn't here . . . .

BENVOLIO: I saw him this morning. I was in a mood. He seemed in a mood too. So we just sorta ignored each other.

MONTAGUE: Yes. He's been really depressed lately. Cries a lot. Closes his curtains during the day and just . . . yeah . . . cries . . . .

BENVOLIO: Do you know why?

MONTAGUE: Nope. We asked, but he wouldn't say.

---

4   A fight that nobody understands anymore. Seriously! Read the entire play! Nowhere does it say why these two are feuding!

Enter ROMEO.

BENVOLIO: Hey, there he is! I'll ask. I'm sure he'll tell me!

MONTAGUE: Excellent! We'll leave you two alone.

Exit MONTAGUE *and* LADY MONTAGUE.

BENVOLIO: Mornin' Cuz.

ROMEO: Is it still morning?

BENVOLIO: Umm. Yeah . . . like nine.

ROMEO: Oh. Well, you know how time flies when you're having fun? When you're sad, the opposite is true.

BENVOLIO: What sadness lengthens your hours?

ROMEO: Love. Love sucks.

BENVOLIO: Oh. That's so sad. Now I'm depressed.

ROMEO: Great! Now I'm even sadder because I made you sad! I'm gonna go cry more!

BENVOLIO: Don't leave. If you do, then you're insulting me! Seriously, who do you love?

ROMEO: A woman.

BENVOLIO: Shocking . . . .

ROMEO: She's pretty.

BENVOLIO: Okay . . . that's good.

ROMEO: No! She's sworn to live as a virgin for her entire life! I love her and I can't ever . . . umm . . . you know. Let's just say she won't open her lap to "saint-seducing gold," if you know what I mean.

BENVOLIO: Okay. Gross. But okay. So just don't think about her.

ROMEO: But then I can't think.

BENVOLIO: Dude. Just check out all the other honeys out there.

ROMEO: No. If I see a hottie, it will just remind me of her.

BENVOLIO: Right . . . I'll take that bet.

They exit.

ACT 1, SCENE 2

Enter CAPULET *and* COUNT PARIS *(the Prince's cousin) mid-conversation.*

CAPULET: . . . so anyway, the Prince says I can't fight Montague, but he can't fight me either. I think we'll make it work.

PARIS: Cool. So, not to change the subject or anything, but . . . I wanna marry your daughter. What do you think?

CAPULET: Well . . . she's only thirteen, so . . . umm . . . how about we wait a year?[5]

PARIS: Nah. Girls younger than her are already moms!

CAPULET: Well, I love my little girl and she is my only child. So I'm gonna say that you have to get her to say yes before I approve. Her choice. But I'll make it easy for you. I'm throwing a party tonight. You're invited. If you see a different girl that you wanna get with, so be it. But if you want my daughter, you can flirt with her and see if she consents. *(calls offstage)* Servant!

SERVINGMAN *enters.*

Here is a guest list for the party tonight. Find these people and invite them.

CAPULET *and* PARIS *exit.*

SERVINGMAN: Dang it. How am I supposed to find these people when I don't know how to read? I'll ask these two guys if they can read!

Enter ROMEO *and* BENVOLIO.

BENVOLIO: I'm telling you man, the best way to get over a girl is to find another one. Rebound!

ROMEO: No! I'm so dramatic! I'm going to say fancy things about how love is a prison and I am trapped and tortured in it![6] *(to* SERVINGMAN*)* Oh hi! What's up?

SERVINGMAN: Do you know how to read?

ROMEO: Yup!

SERVINGMAN: Help?

---

5   !!!

6   Shakespeare spends a lot of time on this point to demonstrate Romeo's extreme immaturity when it comes to love and to show how emotionally dramatic the boy is. Go and read the original text and see how much he whines. I watered it down! He's not exactly the romantic leading man he's thought to be, is he?

ROMEO: It's a guest list: random name, random name, random name, Mercutio, random name, random name, Rosaline, random name, random name. That's quite a list! Where's the party at?

SERVINGMAN: My master's house.

ROMEO: Awesome . . . not helpful.

SERVINGMAN: It's at the Capulet house. So as long as you aren't a Montague, come on down!

Exit SERVINGMAN.

BENVOLIO: Dude! Rosaline, y'know the girl you're crushing on, is going to be at this party.[7] Let's crash it so that you can see her next to some of the honeys I'll show you . . . you'll see she ain't all that.

ROMEO: Impossible. The sun has never seen a girl of Rosaline's hotness.

BENVOLIO: We'll see. Let's do it!

ROMEO: Okay. I'll go. But not to find another girl. Only to bask in Rosaline's beauty one more time.

ROMEO *and* BENVOLIO *exit.*

ACT 1, SCENE 3

Enter LADY CAPULET *and* NURSE.

LADY CAPULET: Hey Nurse, where's my daughter?

NURSE: I dunno. Hey Juliet! Where are you?!

Enter JULIET.

JULIET: I'm right here. Who wants me?

NURSE: Your mom.

JULIET: 'Sup Mom?

LADY CAPULET: You're at a pretty age . . . Nurse, how old is she again?[8]

NURSE: Thirteen. Now I'm going to tell a long-winded, highly repetitive story about how I know her age, which for the most part has nothing to do

---

[7] Whoa! Plot twist! This whole time we assumed Romeo was talking about Juliet! But it's some girl named Rosaline!

[8] She doesn't know her daughter's age . . . mother of the year right here, folks!

with anything.[9]

LADY CAPULET: Shut up, Nurse.

NURSE: I'm sorry, but it's a really funny story about how my husband got Juliet to inadvertently make a sex joke when she was really little!

JULIET: Seriously, Nurse. Shut up.

NURSE: Okay. I'm done.

LADY CAPULET: Juliet, how do you feel about marriage?

JULIET: Meh. Haven't really thought about it.

LADY CAPULET: Well, think about it now. Count Paris wants to marry you!

NURSE: OMG! He is sooo hot!

LADY CAPULET: Oh yeah! He's like a book just missing a beautiful cover . . . you could be that cover! What do you think?

NURSE: And babies!!!

JULIET: I'll take a look at him, but only because you're asking me to.

Enter SERVINGMAN.

SERVINGMAN: Madam, things are getting crazy downstairs and the guests are arriving.

LADY CAPULET: On our way. Juliet, the count is waiting.

NURSE: Go Juliet. Seek happy nights for your happy days![10]

They exit.

ACT 1, SCENE 4

Enter ROMEO, MERCUTIO *(another cousin of the Prince)*, BENVOLIO, *and a bunch of other guys.*

ROMEO: Sooo, should we just crash the party? Or apologize when we enter?

BENVOLIO: Crash it, dude! We're gonna dance with the hot ladies, and boom! We outta there!

ROMEO: Ugh. I'm depressed. I'll just carry the torch.

---

9   You're welcome.
10   Sex!

MERCUTIO: No, Romeo. You must dance!

ROMEO: No. You have dancing soles. I have a soul of lead.[11]

MERCUTIO: Come on! You're a lover! Borrow Cupid's wings and fly!

ROMEO: No. I have been shot with Cupid's arrow and I am sinking.

MERCUTIO: But what you talk of is love, a very tender thing!

ROMEO: No. Love sucks. It hurts and pricks like a thorn.

MERCUTIO: Dude, if love is rough with you, be rough with love. Find a girl and have a one-night stand! That'll cure you!

BENVOLIO: Come on guys! We're going to be late!

ROMEO: No. I am overdramatic and whiny and I'm done with all this. I don't want to go.

MERCUTIO: Why not?

ROMEO: I had a dream.

MERCUTIO: Me too!

ROMEO: What was yours?

MERCUTIO: That dreamers often lie.

ROMEO: Sometimes dreams come true!

MERCUTIO: Ah. I see you have been visited by Queen Mab, a fairy who influences people's dreams. I could tell you all about this fairy queen, in extremely precise detail, but I won't because nobody really wants to hear that.[12]

ROMEO: Man, that is some BS.

MERCUTIO: True. Because I'm talking about dreams! They are nothing but children of the idle brain—a.k.a. BS. Don't pay any attention to them!

BENVOLIO: Seriously guys! We're missing the food!

ROMEO: Huh. I have a bad feeling about this. I feel like there is something hanging in the stars . . . that something is going to begin tonight that will ultimately lead me to my own death . . . . Oh well, that's fate for you! Let's go, loverboys!

---

[11]   Ha! Puns are fun!
[12]   You're welcome.

10

BENVOLIO: Yeah!

They exit.

ACT 1, SCENE 5

FIRST SERVINGMAN: Where the heck is Potpan?! Why isn't he helping clean up? Who does he think he is?

SECOND SERVINGMAN: No kidding! It sucks when it falls to one or two guys to do everything!

FIRST SERVINGMAN: Move those stools and remove the sideboard. Grab that plate! Hey, save me some of that cheese! . . . Anthony and Potpan!

THIRD SERVINGMAN (POTPAN): 'Sup?

FIRST SERVINGMAN: Dude, they have been searching, asking, looking, and calling for you in the great chamber!

THIRD SERVINGMAN: Seriously? We can't be there and here all at once! Oh well. Keep up your spirits, boys. The survivor of this will take all. Winning!

Servingmen move aside. Enter CAPULET *and his family, all of the guests and gentlewomen,* ROMEO, MERCUTIO, BENVOLIO, *and all the other maskers.*

CAPULET: Welcome, gentlemen! Ladies that don't have corns on their toes will now dance with you all! —Haha! Ladies, who will now refuse to dance? 'Cos if you do, we will all just assume you can't dance because you have corns on your toes and that is just nasty! —Welcome, gentlemen. I remember back in the day when I wore a mask at these masquerade balls. I would whisper into all the girls' ears. Oh, but those days are long gone now. I'm too old. Now it is your turn gentlemen! —Musicians, play some music!

Music plays and everyone starts dancing.

Make room! —Dance girls! —Servants! We need more light, ya idiots! And move the tables! And extinguish the fire, it's too damn hot in here! Seriously, you guys are worthless! —Ah, this is fun! *(turns to Capulet's cousin)* No, stay seated my good cousin. Our dancing days are over. We're too old! How long ago was it when we last did this?

CAPULET'S COUSIN: Oh man . . . thirty years!

CAPULET: No way! It can't be that long ago! It was at Lucentio's wedding. That was only twenty-five years ago!

CAPULET'S COUSIN: No, it's more! His son is older than that! His son is thirty!

11

CAPULET: What?! His son was just a kid like two years ago!

ROMEO *approaches the first servingman.*

ROMEO *(to the first servingman)*: Hey man, who is that girl dancing with that lucky guy over there? *(Motions toward Juliet.)*

FIRST SERVINGMAN: I don't know, sir.

ROMEO: Dang. She is so hot; she is teaching torches to burn bright! She is like a jewel in an ear. Her beauty is too much for this world. She looks like a snowy white dove dancing among a bunch of crows. When the song is done, I will watch where she goes to stand and then take her blessed hand in mine. Oh man! Did my heart love 'til now? I know that I have never seen true beauty 'til this night![13]

TYBALT *recognizes Romeo's voice and is pissed!*

TYBALT: That voice . . . oh hell no! It's a Montague! *(to Page)* Go get my sword, boy! *(PAGE exits.)* Oh no he didn't! He did not just come to our party to sneer at our fun. Now by the stock and honor of my kin, to strike him dead I hold it not a sin. Imma gonna kill him!

CAPULET *sees the angry Tybalt and approaches him.*

CAPULET: Hey fam! Why are you so angry? Where are you storming off to?

TYBALT: Uncle! That is a Montague, our enemy! A villain who has crashed our party to ruin it!

CAPULET: Who is it? Romeo?

TYBALT: Yes. That damn Romeo . . . I hate him!

CAPULET: Oh, Nephew, leave him alone. He is acting like a gentleman and to tell you the truth, everyone in Verona says he is a good and virtuous young man. I would not for all the money in this town insult or embarrass him here in my own home. So relax. Ignore him. It is what I want, and if you respect me, you will turn that frown upside down and have a good time. Act like you are at a party, man!

TYBALT: No. My frown is perfect when a loser like him is a guest. I will not endure him!

CAPULET: He shall be endured! What? Who's the master here, you or me? Huh?! Are you really going to kill somebody in the middle of my party?! You'll

---

13   Just wanna point out that this is Benvolio's ultimate "told-ya-so" moment. He knows his cousin well.

cause a riot among my guests!

TYBALT: But Uncle, it's a shame . . .

CAPULET: Stop! You're being a butt. Is that what you are? You're gonna get hurt. Don't you go against me, boy. I'll make you quiet!

Starts to walk away.

(to guests) Well done! *(to servants)* More light, more light!

TYBALT: This makes my blood boil. Oooo, I'm pissed. I will withdraw . . . but this intrusion, now seeming so sweet, will be avenged.

TYBALT *exits.*

The song ends and ROMEO *moves to* JULIET *and takes her hand.*[14]

ROMEO: If I dirty with my unworthy hand
Your hand, a shrine which men journey to pray,
Then I have sinned, and if you will demand,
My lips will repent with a kiss today.

JULIET: Good sir, you insult your own hand too much.
This devotion to me, your shrine, is shown
With hands. When it is a saint's hands you touch,
Then you can call a "Palmer's Kiss" your own!

ROMEO: Yes, dear, but don't saints also have lips too?

JULIET: Of course, sir! Lips they must use in prayer!

ROMEO: Oh then, dear saint, let lips do what hands do!
They both pray, but they kiss too, Lady Fair!

JULIET: A saint does not accept or deny this.

ROMEO: Then grant my prayer with this holy first kiss!

ROMEO *kisses* JULIET.[15]

And with that kiss, because you are a shrine and saint in this little metaphor, I have purged my sin!

JULIET: Wait. That means your sin is now on MY lips? Not cool.

---

14   Romeo, feeling super passionate, starts laying down some poetry. (This convo takes the form of a sonnet. It is a type of poem like the prologue . . . look it up.) The poem culminates in their first kiss.

15   Oooo! And this ends the sonnet.

ROMEO: What? No! I cannot allow your lips to carry my sin! I take it back!

ROMEO *kisses* JULIET *again.*[16]

JULIET: Wow . . . boy knows how to kiss!

ROMEO *gives a wink, wink.*

NURSE: Madam, your mother needs to talk to you!

JULIET *moves toward Lady Capulet.*

ROMEO *(to Nurse)*: Who is her mother?

NURSE: Her mother is the lady of the house, THE Lady Capulet! She's a wise and virtuous mother. I nursed the young lady you were just talking to! And let me tell you, the man who gets her is gonna be RICH! Haha!

NURSE *walks away.*

ROMEO: Oh God! She is a Capulet? Dang it! My love, my life is my enemy?! NOOOO!!!

BENVOLIO: Come on, let's get outta here. This place is dead anyway.

ROMEO: Huh? Oh . . . okay . . . yeah. So's my heart . . . .

CAPULET: What? No! Gentlemen don't leave yet! The party is still going strong! We're just getting star . . . *(LADY CAPULET whispers to him)* . . . oh really? It's that late? Oh . . . okay. Good night all! I guess it's bedtime! Good night!

Everybody starts to exit, except JULIET *and her nurse.*

JULIET: Hey Nurse, come here. Who is that gentleman over there? *(She points to some random guy so Nurse doesn't suspect anything.)*

NURSE: Tiberio's son.

JULIET: And that boy going out the door? *(points to another random dude)*

NURSE: That would be Petruchio.

JULIET: Okay. And how about that boy there who wouldn't dance?[17] *(pointing to Romeo)*

NURSE: I don't know.

---

16   And . . . passionately . . . dang, this boy has some game.
17   Oooo!

14

JULIET: Could you please go find out? *(NURSE goes and asks someone.)* If he turns out to be married, I am seriously going to die.

NURSE *returns.*

NURSE: His name is Romeo and he is a Montague. You know, the only son of your great ENEMY!

JULIET: My only love was born of my only hate;
I saw him too early, and now it is too late.
It is not fair to me
That I have fallen for my enemy.

NURSE: I'm sorry, what was that? I didn't hear you.

JULIET: Oh . . . umm. Nothing. Just some poem I heard earlier today. Forget I said anything.

Someone offstage calls for Juliet.

NURSE: Oh well. Let's go. All the guests are gone.

They exit.

END OF ACT 1

ACT 2

PROLOGUE[18]

Enter CHORUS

CHORUS:
Now his love for Rosaline is dying
And now a new affection takes its place.
Things for which earlier he was crying,
Compared to Juliet, isn't a fair race.

Romeo loves again, and her love grows.
Both of them drawn to each other's good looks.
But now he must be given favor from his foes
And she must steal love's bait from risky hooks.

Because he is a foe, he may not be
Able to whisper vows into her ear.
And she, as much in love, wanting to see
Her man, her ability even less clear.

But passion lends power to him and her
Mixing difficulties with great pleasure.

ACT 2, SCENE 1

Enter ROMEO, *alone.*

ROMEO: How can I leave when my love and my heart is here?

ROMEO *hides behind a bush or wall or tree or something.*

Enter BENVOLIO *and* MERCUTIO.

BENVOLIO: Romeo! Romeo! Where are you?! Romeo!

MERCUTIO: I'm sure he went home to bed.

BENVOLIO: No. He ran this way and jumped over this wall. Help me find him!

MERCUTIO: Nah. I'll conjure him. I'll make him come to ME! I summon

---

18   Again, as mentioned before, this is NOT the original text. However, as I rewrote this prologue, I kept it a sonnet.

you, Romeo! Madman! Lover! Appear before me! Say something! Sigh and I'll be satisfied! Say something about love, your favorite topic! Come to me! . . . Huh. It's not working. I must do more . . . *(snicker)* . . . Romeo! I conjure you by Rosaline's bright eyes, her sexy face, her suckable . . . kissable lips! I summon you by her fine foot . . . her long leg . . . her quivering thigh . . . and her . . . uh . . . the regions that come between those thighs! Come out!

BENVOLIO: Dude, you are going to piss him off!

MERCUTIO: Nah! Saying these things won't anger him . . . but you know what would? It would anger him to continue conjuring spirits. To raise a spirit in his lady's "circle" and let that spirit stand there until she "laid" it and "conjured" it down! Now THAT would anger him! Ha![19]

BENVOLIO: Come on. He's hiding in the trees and wants to pout in the dark of night. It's kinda his thing.

MERCUTIO: Yeah. He's probably sitting under a medlar tree wishing his lady were that kind of fruit. 'Cos you know, medlar fruit has a pit that looks like a butthole, so people call them "open-arses"! Romeo! I wish she was an open-arse so you could "pop her in the pear" and stop this! Romeo! Good night! It's cold and I'm going to bed! Let's go, Benvolio.

BENVOLIO: Yeah. It's stupid to look for someone who doesn't want to be found. Let's go.

BENVOLIO *and* MERCUTIO *exit.*

ACT 2, SCENE 2 *(The Balcony Scene!)*

ROMEO *comes out of hiding.*

ROMEO: Only someone who has never been in love jokes about it like that. Anyway, I don't really care what he says about Rosaline anymore.

Enter JULIET *above.*[20]

(aside)[21] But soft, what light through yonder window breaks? Wait, what did

---

[19]   This is a play on words using the conjuring of dead spirits in a circle of people, or symbols, as a metaphor for having sex with Rosaline. He is trying to anger Romeo so he will come out of hiding to defend his lady, which obviously doesn't work because Romeo doesn't care about Rosaline anymore, but Mercutio doesn't know that.

[20]   On a balcony! Or not—it is really up to the director. Oh, and she has absolutely NO clue that Romeo is right below her.

[21]   Meaning Juliet can't hear him say any of this.

I say? Huh. Oh well. Hey! What light is that coming from that window? Is it her room?! Oh man! I'm about to get all metaphorical again, 'cos that's what I do! That light is the East and Juliet is the sun! Arise fair sun! Kill off the moon who is jealous of your beauty! Oh it is my lady! Oh it is my love! Oh how I wish she knew how I felt! She speaks and yet she says nothing . . . it is her eyes. Her eyes speak! I should say something! No. Her eyes are not speaking to me. It's almost like two stars in heaven had to go somewhere and asked her eyes to take their places in the sky until they return. If that happened, her eyes would be so bright in the sky that birds would start to sing because they would think it were day! Oh . . . look how she rests her cheek on her hand . . . . Oh how I wish I were a glove on that hand so that I could be touching that cheek!

JULIET: *(sighs)* Ay me!

ROMEO: *(aside)*[22] She speaks! Oh speak again, bright angel! You truly are an angel because you are like a winged messenger of heaven soaring above me![23]

JULIET: Oh Romeo, Romeo, wherefore art thou Romeo? [24] Why did I have to fall for Romeo?! Why not Tiberio or Petruchio or Paris? There would be no issues then! Why Romeo? Oh, deny your father and refuse your name, or if you can't do that, swear that you love me and I'll no longer be a Capulet!

ROMEO: *(aside)*[25] Should I keep listening to this? Or should I say something to let her know I'm here?[26]

JULIET: It is his name that is my enemy, not him. He is just him, not a Montague. What is Montague? It isn't a hand or a foot or arm or face . . . or any other part belonging to a man. *(giggle, giggle)* Oh, be some other name! What's in a name? A rose by any other name would smell just as sweet! So the same goes for Romeo! If his name were something other than Romeo, he would still be the perfect man that he is, even without the name! So Romeo, throw away your name and for it, you can have me!

---

22   Because he is being a creeper and not letting her know that he is watching her.

23   For those of you keeping score at home, Juliet has now been compared to a jewel, a dove, a shrine, a saint, the sun, her eyes to stars, and now she is an angel. Wow.

24   In other words: Oh Romeo, Romeo, WHY are you Romeo? Not where!

25   Because, no, he still has not let her know that he is totally eavesdropping on her.

26   Obviously he just keeps quiet and continues listening . . . creeper.

ROMEO: *(unable to contain himself any longer, jumping out of hiding)* I take you at your word! Just call me Love and I will be baptized again. And from now on, I will never be called Romeo!

JULIET: *(taken aback and shocked at this random dude in the shadows that jumped out at her and started yelling stuff)* What the ...! Who's out there in the shadows listening to me!

ROMEO: I don't know how to tell you who I am since my name, dear saint, is hateful to me and an enemy to you. If I had my name written on a piece of paper, I would tear the word!

JULIET: I haven't heard even a hundred words of your voice, yet I already know it! Aren't you Romeo, and a Montague?

ROMEO: Neither, fair maid, if you dislike them.

JULIET: How did you get here, and why? The orchard walls are high and hard to climb and this place is death, considering who you are, if any of my family finds you here.

ROMEO: With love's light wings did I fly over the walls, for no wall can hold love out! And love will attempt whatever is possible for it to do, so your family cannot stop me!

JULIET: Umm ... okay ... but if they see you, they will murder you.

ROMEO: Oh honey, there is more danger in your eye than twenty of their swords. But your love makes me invincible!

JULIET: Alrighty then. I still don't want them to find you here.

ROMEO: I have the darkness of night to hide me from their eyes. But if you don't love me, then I want them to find me and kill me right here and now. I would rather die now than live another second without your love.

JULIET: But how did you find my window?

ROMEO: By love! They say love is blind, so I lent him my eyes! Truth is, if you were on the farthest shore on the farthest sea, I would come to find you.

JULIET: It's dark, so I know you can't see me very well. But if you could, you would see that I am blushing because of what you heard me say tonight. I wish I could follow the proper formalities. I gladly would deny what I said, but that is not possible now. Do you love me? I know you will say yes, and I will take your word for it, but the truth is you may be lying and just saying it because of what you heard me say. You may say yes just to get into my ... uh ... y'know ... um, to get whatever you want from me. So please, Romeo, if you say it, say it faithfully and honestly. Don't play with my heart. Or, if you think I am too easy, I will play hard to get. I will tell you "no" and force you to pursue me and court me the proper way, but I would rather not go through all that. Honestly, I like you too much. And because of that you may think that I am immodest or flighty or "easy." But trust me, I will prove more faithful and loyal to you than other girls who are better at being coy and "hard to get." I must admit that I should have been like that. I should have made you pursue me, but I just realized my true love and passion for you and I didn't realize you were listening to me. So, forgive me for that, but do not mistake the speed at which you won me over to indicate a light love.

ROMEO: My lady, I swear by the blessed moon . . .

JULIET: Wait. The moon? Seriously? The thing that is constantly changing? Please don't swear by something that is always changing, because that might mean your love will change as well.

ROMEO: Well, what shall I swear by?

JULIET: Don't swear at all. Or if you do, swear by your own gracious self and I will believe you!

ROMEO: Okay! I swear by . . .

JULIET: Wait. Stop. Just don't swear. At all. Look. I'm loving this. I really am. But this is moving WAAAY too fast for me. So good night. This love is just like a flower budding, and in time, this may become a beautiful thing when we meet again. But right now, it is too fast. Good night.[27]

ROMEO: Will you leave me so unsatisfied?

JULIET: Umm . . . what satisfaction can you have tonight?

ROMEO: Your faithful vow of love in exchange for mine.

JULIET: I already gave it to you! But I wish I had it back.

ROMEO: You would take it back? Why?

JULIET: So I could give it to you again! My love is like the sea! It is boundless and deep! The more love I give to you, the more I have to give! I have an infinite amount of love![28]

NURSE *calls for Juliet from offstage.*

Oh no! I hear the nurse calling for me . . . in a minute, Nurse! Sweet Montague,

---

27   Finally, one of these two shows some restraint and common sense!

28   Okay, nevermind about the whole restraint and common sense thing.

stay right here. I'll be right back!

JULIET *exits into her room.*

ROMEO: Oh my God! This is the greatest night of my life! But since it is night, is it possible this is all just a dream? Is it all too good to be true?

JULIET *returns.*

JULIET: Okay Romeo, I've just got a few seconds, then you have to leave. If you truly love me, are honorable, and want to get married, give me a message tomorrow through someone I will send to you.[29] Tell her where and when the marriage ceremony is to take place and I will be there. Then I will follow you throughout the world.

NURSE *(from offstage)*: Madam!

JULIET *(to Nurse)*: Be right there! *(to Romeo)* But if you do not mean well, I beg you . . .

NURSE *(from offstage)*: Madam!

JULIET *(to Nurse)*: Coming! *(to Romeo)* Please leave me alone in my despair and never speak to me again. I will send someone to you tomorrow!

ROMEO: You make my soul joyful![30]

JULIET: Good night! A thousand times good night!

JULIET *exits into her bedroom.*

ROMEO: I love you.

ROMEO *turns and starts to leave.* JULIET *returns again.*

JULIET: Psst. Romeo! Psst. God I love saying his name and calling him to me!

ROMEO: Is that my soul calling my name? Hearing you say my name is music to my ears!

JULIET: Romeo.

ROMEO: Yes, my dear?

---

29   Wait . . . what?! That escalated quickly!
30   Okay. So, Romeo is down for marriage. After one night. Literally an hour. This is why Shakespeare had to establish Romeo as an emotionally immature and extremely dramatic loverboy. It makes this impulsive decision consistent to his character. Still crazy though!

JULIET: What time tomorrow should I send my messenger to you?

ROMEO: Nine.

JULIET: I will not fail. It seems like twenty years 'til then! . . . Romeo! Wait . . . I forgot why I called you back again.

ROMEO: Okay. Well, I will just stand here until you remember! Then I can stay with you!

JULIET: Then I will just keep forgetting so you stay here with me, because I love your company!

ROMEO: Well, then I'll just stay here so you keep forgetting and this spot will be my new home![31]

JULIET: Oh, but it's almost morning! I want you to leave, but I want you to be like a pet bird whose foot I tie a string to so it can only fly so far before I pull it back to me!

ROMEO: I wish I were your bird!

JULIET: Sweet! So do I! Yet if you were, I would probably kill you with too much loving![32] Good night! Parting is such sweet sorrow that I will keep saying "good night" until tomorrow!

JULIET *exits.*

ROMEO: Sleep well, my love, and peace be in your heart. I can't sleep now. I need to go to my friar's place and ask for his help and tell him all about this night!

ROMEO *exits.*

ACT 2, SCENE 3

Enter FRIAR LAWRENCE *with a basket.*

FRIAR LAWRENCE: What a beautiful dawn! The sun is just rising to start another lovely day. Time for me to fill up this basket with weeds, roots, plants, and flowers. It is crazy how much can be contained in these little things. Some of these are medicine. Some are poison. Some are both, depending on how they are used. Even in this little plant here. There is good and bad—just like in men. And when the bad takes over, the plant will die—as will the man. I love

---

31   This is the Shakespeare version of that annoying couple who talks on the phone and playfully argues about who should hang up first . . . gag.

32   Anybody else finding this exchange a bit, oh I don't know . . . creepy?

a good metaphor! I have been studying the medicinal applications of plants for a long time. I wonder if this expertise will play a role in some future events. Hmm.

Enter ROMEO.

ROMEO: Good Morning, Father.

FRIAR LAWRENCE: Bless you child. Who is calling on me so early? Young man, there are only two reasons you would be up talking to me this early. Either you have something disturbing your mind and forcing you to get out of bed early or, if not that, you have not gone to bed yet!

ROMEO: The second one! But trust me, I am so rested!

FRIAR LAWRENCE: God pardon sin! Were you with Rosaline?!

ROMEO: Who? No! Not Rosaline. I'm sooo over her!

FRIAR LAWRENCE: That's my good boy. Then where have you been?

ROMEO: I'll tell thee ere thou ask it me again.
I have been feasting with mine enemy,
Where on a sudden one hath wounded me
That's by me wounded. Both our remedies
Within thy help and holy physic lies.
I bear no hatred, blessed man, for, lo,
My intercession likewise steads my foe.[33]

FRIAR LAWRENCE: I have no idea what you just said.[34] Be clear and speak in plain language. If I can't understand your confession, I can't tell you how to proceed. Try again.

ROMEO: Sorry. Let me try to be clearer. My heart is now set on the fair daughter of rich Capulet! She loves me as much as I love her. Our hearts are combined, and now you must combine our souls. How we met and fell in love, I'll explain later, but this is what I am here to ask: that you agree to marry Juliet and me today!

FRIAR LAWRENCE: Holy Saint Francis! What a change is this! Is Rosaline, that you loved so dear, so soon forgotten? If so, then you did not love her with your heart but with your eyes. Good Lord, how much time did you spend wiping tears from your cheeks?! How many tears were wasted?! Your sighs are still lingering in the air! Your groans and cries still ringing in my ears! Look! Right

---

33   This is from the actual text: act 2, scene 3, lines 52–58.
34   Just like the rest of us!

here! There is still the stain of an old tear that hasn't washed off yet! All of that for Rosaline! And now all of that has changed? Please!^{35}

ROMEO: But you scolded me often for loving Rosaline.

FRIAR LAWRENCE: For lusting, not for loving.

ROMEO: You told me to bury my love for her!

FRIAR LAWRENCE: Not to just unbury it for the first pretty girl you see!

ROMEO: I beg you, please stop. I love Juliet now. And she loves me back. Rosaline didn't.

FRIAR LAWRENCE: That's because she knew you did not know what love was. But come young waverer. Follow me. I will actually help you. I will agree to this marriage for one reason (and it ain't about love). I will do this in the hopes that this marriage will turn your families' hatred for each other into pure love and end the feud that has been tearing this city apart.^{36}

ROMEO: Awesome! Let's go! Hurry!

FRIAR LAWRENCE: Wisely and slow. Those who run fast do stumble.

They exit.

ACT 2, SCENE 4

Enter BENVOLIO *and* MERCUTIO.

MERCUTIO: Where is Romeo? Did he come home last night?

BENVOLIO: Nope. I spoke with his servant.

MERCUTIO: It's that Rosaline's fault. That hard-hearted wench tortures him and drives him crazy.

BENVOLIO: Tybalt, the nephew of old Capulet, sent a letter to Romeo's house.

MERCUTIO: A challenge to a duel?! Hell yeah!

BENVOLIO: Hell yes, Romeo will answer it!

MERCUTIO: So? Anybody who knows how to write can answer a letter!

---

35   Thank you, Friar Lawrence, for being a voice of reason!
36   Well, there goes the whole voice-of-reason thing. Sure! Let's secretly wed two teenagers, whose families hate each other, without the families' knowledge! What could possibly go wrong?!

BENVOLIO: You know what I mean! Romeo will take on Tybalt! He'll accept the challenge!

MERCUTIO: No. Unfortunately, Romeo is already dead. Rosaline has already killed him. Cupid's arrow already shot him in the heart. Right now, he ain't got the balls to fight Tybalt.

BENVOLIO: What?! No way. He can still take Tybalt . . . right? Is Tybalt . . . good or something?

MERCUTIO: Oh . . . he's good. He's the king of fencing etiquette. He fights like a song. He keeps proper time and distance and proportion. He rests and then one *(a slashing motion)*, two *(a parry)*, and three *(fake stabs Benvolio in the chest)*. And you're dead. He can carve a button off your shirt. Oh . . . he's good. He trains at the best fencing school. And he will unleash the passado, the punto reverso, and the hay![37]

BENVOLIO: The what?

MERCUTIO: Oh just the annoying terminology of the snobs in those schools. They think they're so cool. Pretentious butts is what they are. It just pisses me off.

Enter ROMEO.

BENVOLIO: Here comes Romeo! He's alive!

MERCUTIO: Yup. Here he comes. And he looks spent. I bet he's been up all night, writing poetry about his girl. Dang, you'd think she was hotter than Laura.[38] Even more, I'd bet he would think she was a kitchen slut compared to Rosaline. Yeah. And Dido was a drag, Cleopatra a harlot, Helen and Hera were just whores compared to his girl.[39] Seriously . . . *(to Romeo)* Signior Romeo, bonjour! There's a French welcome for your French BS. You gave us the counterfeit last night.

ROMEO: Morning guys. What counterfeit are you talking about?

MERCUTIO: Seriously dude? You ditched us last night. Are you dense?

ROMEO: Oh. Yeah, sorry about that. But I was tending to something very

---

37   Fencing terms.
38   From Petrarch.
39   These are all legendary women who were known for their beauty.

important, and in this case, I think I am allowed to strain courtesy.[40]

MERCUTIO: Oh. Right. You're so important. I'd say it was less "courtesy" and more bowing with your legs.

ROMEO: You mean I curtsy?[41]

MERCUTIO: Ding, ding, ding! We have a winner!

ROMEO: How courteous of you.

MERCUTIO: Dude. I am the most courteous man you will ever meet.

ROMEO: You are, huh? Well, I see your courtesy and raise you one![42]

MERCUTIO:[43] Ohhh dang! Look who thinks he's tough! Try to challenge me, BOY, and you will wear your "shoes" out.[44]

ROMEO: Says the guy whose last "running" partner told me your "shoes" are worn out after only one lap![45]

MERCUTIO: Oh shi—! Dang! Benvolio come between us! Protect me from this punk!

ROMEO: Come back Mercutio! Otherwise, I declare victory!

MERCUTIO: Nah. No way. When you are on your game, I'm no match for you. It would be a wild goose chase for me to try.

ROMEO: Ha. You ARE the goose!

---

40   The following is an exchange between Romeo, Mercutio, and Benvolio that is used to show why cool guys like Mercutio and Benvolio have spent so much time trying to cheer up Romeo. Because, when he is not wallowing in self-pitying hopeless romanticism, he is actually a really witty, fun, and cool guy. This battle of wits is to show he is back to "normal" now that he is with Juliet. Unfortunately, this exchange has not aged well and is filled with terrible puns about shoes and geese that most modern audiences (especially teenagers) will not follow easily and more than likely will not find funny in the least. But back in Shakespeare's time—you will just have to believe me—this was hilarious. I have done my best to try and make it somewhat fun to read. Enjoy!

41   A woman's bow.

42   If you want to go to Shakespeare, this is where they discuss shoes ... but if you want to have Romeo give a motion to "raising" something other than his shoe, go for it!

43   Realizing now that Romeo is engaging with him and not griping about love.

44   Again, this can mean he is wearing out his shoes ... or something else.

45   Again ... is this literally about shoes or ... something else?

MERCUTIO: What? No! Dude, I will smack you!

ROMEO: Oooo, I'm so scared. No please, goosey, don't hit me!

MERCUTIO: Man, you gonna make me salty!

ROMEO: Good! A goose needs some salt! Goose.

MERCUTIO: Oh now that's a stretch man.

ROMEO: Of course I had to stretch it. You're a fat . . . goose!

(At this point, the two boys break into laughter and high five, or hug, or both.)

MERCUTIO: He's BACK! Isn't this better than groaning for love? Now you're sociable! Now you're Romeo! Running around looking for love is like an idiot jester running around looking for a hole to hide his baton in![46]

BENVOLIO: No! Stop right there!

MERCUTIO: Why? Why should I stop my tale now?[47] I was just getting started!

BENVOLIO: 'Cos I know you, and you would have made your "tale" longer than it has any business being.

MERCUTIO: What? No! Not me! It would have been short! I would have simply finished when my "tale" was exhausted and then quickly left as soon as my business was be done![48]

Enter NURSE *and* PETER *(her servant).*

ROMEO: Oooo, check out this beauty! A sail! I see a sail![49]

MERCUTIO: Two of them!

NURSE: Peter.

PETER: Yes, Madam.

NURSE: Give me my fan, Peter.

---

46   Yes! More sex metaphors!

47   Tail?

48   Benvolio and Romeo simply smile and shake their heads. Mercutio makes everything dirty.

49   Romeo obviously doesn't recognize the nurse yet, because he is insulting her looks and size (being an jerk, really), and that would not be a smart move as this is the woman who basically raised Juliet and is someone she loves dearly.

MERCUTIO: Yes, please Peter, give her the fan because she can use it to cover her face! The fan is way prettier!

NURSE: Good morning, gentlemen.

MERCUTIO: And a good evening to you, fair gentlewoman.

NURSE: Good evening? Is it evening?

MERCUTIO: Of course. The hand of the clock is now upon the prick of noon![50]

NURSE: What the—?! Get away from me! What kind of man are you?!

ROMEO: A man that even God is ashamed of.

NURSE: Haha! That's funny. Well, can any of you gentlemen tell me where I may find the young Romeo?

ROMEO: Huh? Oh, well that would be me!

NURSE: If you are him, then I need to talk to you . . . in private.

MERCUTIO: Whoa! Is she a bawd?![51]

ROMEO: What? Mercutio, no. Stop.[52]

MERCUTIO: Don't worry, buddy! What I mean is that she is a hare![53] *(to Nurse)* Just remember, my lovely lady, that a hare is a very good meat to eat during Lent![54] *(back to Romeo)* Romeo! Are you coming to your father's house for dinner? Let's go.

ROMEO: I'll meet you there. Go ahead.

MERCUTIO: Cool. Farewell, ancient lady! Farewell lady, lady, lady!

MERCUTIO *and* BENVOLIO *exit.*

NURSE: Ugh. Who was that disgusting man?

---

50   Mercutio does something extremely rude here. He can either grab his crotch, take the nurse's hand and place it on his crotch, or do a pelvic thrust on the word "prick." He has to do something nasty based on the nurse's reaction.

51   A bawd is a female pimp . . . but in another dialect, it can also mean a hare, which is a large rabbit.

52   Romeo has just realized who the nurse is and is mortified at what his buddy is saying/doing to her.

53   Sure he does.

54   At that, he probably winks or licks his lips at her or something . . . eww! Nurse is disgusted.

ROMEO: A man, Nurse, that loves to hear himself talk and will say more in a minute than he will ever actually do in a month.

NURSE: Oooh, if he says anything else to me, I'll take him out! And if I can't, I'll find someone who can! That knave. I'm not one of his flirty girls! *(to Peter)* Peter! And you just stood there and let him use me for his pleasure!

PETER: Uh . . . I didn't see anyone using you for pleasure! *(snicker)* Oh, I mean . . . yeah. Yeah, if I had, then you know my sword would have been out and I would defend you! I don't shy away from fights . . . you know, if it is for a good reason . . . and um, as long as the law is on my side, and . . .

NURSE: Oh, shut up. You're useless. Ugh. Every part of me quivers, I'm so triggered. What a knave! *(to Romeo)* Now sir. I need a word. My young lady asked me to find you. But before this goes any further, let me first tell you: if you should lead her into a fool's paradise, or you treat her poorly or cheat on her because you know that she is young and innocent, or if you break her heart in any way, it would be a horrible thing to do and there is a special place in Hell for scoundrels who do such things.

ROMEO: Nurse. Please, recommend me to your lady. I protest to you . . .

NURSE: Oh wonderful! That is excellent! I will tell her! She will be so joyful!

ROMEO: Huh? What are you going to tell her? I haven't said anything yet.

NURSE: Just that you do protest! And that is a gentleman-like offer![55]

ROMEO: Umm. Okay. Whatever. Nurse, tell her to go to confession at church and there, in Friar Lawrence's room, she will be absolved and married. Here is some money for your help. *(offering her money)*

NURSE: No sir, not a penny!

ROMEO: Please take it!

NURSE: This afternoon? She will be there!

ROMEO: Wonderful! Oh, Nurse, please stick around for a bit. Stand behind this church wall. My servant will be here within an hour and will give you a rope ladder. Have Juliet hang it from her balcony and it will be my "Stairway to Heaven" to her room tonight! Thank you so much. Farewell, and tell Juliet I love her.

NURSE: God bless you! Oh Romeo, wait!

ROMEO: What is it?

---

55   She has confused the word "protest" with "propose."

NURSE: Is your man trustworthy?

ROMEO: He's as true as steel.

NURSE: Okay. Also, you should know that there is another man in the picture. His name is Paris, and he is also pursuing Juliet. Now don't you worry. She has no interest in him at all. In fact, when I tell her that he is actually more of a proper match than you, she gets very angry with me. She would rather date a toad than him. But you should know he is involved. Also, don't Rosemary and Romeo begin with the same letter?

ROMEO: Um. Yeah. Both with an R.

NURSE: Oh good! That's the dog's name! At least I think it is . . . wait . . . maybe it isn't. Is it a different name? It would be good if it was, because Juliet loves that dog and that would be a good sign.

ROMEO: Okay . . . tell Juliet I love her. Goodbye.

NURSE: Yes. A thousand times goodbye! Peter!

PETER: Yes, Madam.

NURSE: Time to go.

They exit.

ACT 2, SCENE 5

JULIET: Where is the nurse?! I sent her to find Romeo at nine. She said she'd be back in half an hour. That was three hours ago! It's noon! Maybe she can't find him. No, that can't be it. She is just lame. If only she moved at the speed of love's angels. She would be ten times faster! But no. She's old and sometimes old people act like they're already dead, and move about that fast.

Enter NURSE and PETER.

Oh God, she's here! *(to Nurse)* Oh my Nurse, my lovely Nurse, what news do you have? Did you meet him? Send your servant away!

NURSE: Peter, go wait outside.

PETER *exits.*

JULIET: Okay Nurse. Spill it . . . wait, why do you look sad? If you have bad news, then tell it happily so it doesn't seem so bad. And if your news is good, then you shame it by telling it to me with such a sour face!

NURSE: I'm tired! Jeez. Give me a sec, will ya? My bones ache! That was a long walk!

JULIET: Oh come on! I wish you had MY bones and I had your news! Please tell me what happened!

NURSE: My lord, why are you in such a rush? Can't you chill out for a minute? Can't you see I'm out of breath?

JULIET: How can you be out of breath when you have the breath to tell me that you are out of breath?! You could have told me the news a dozen times by now instead of all these excuses about why you haven't told me! Can you please at least just tell me this: is it good or bad?

NURSE: Well, first let me just say that you don't know how to choose a man. Romeo? Nah. Not him. Although, I must admit, he has a very pretty face, and woo-hoo what a body! Rawr! However, he is not the most courteous young man, but he seems like a nice guy. Anyways, what's a girl gonna do? Have you eaten yet?

JULIET: What? No, I haven't eaten! I knew all of that before! What does he say about our marriage?

NURSE: Oh my head hurts! And my back! My poor back! Oh, how it aches! Shame on you for sending an old woman like me out like this![56]

JULIET: I'm sorry, okay? I'm sorry you hurt! But please, PLEASE, will you just tell me what he said? I'm dying here!

NURSE: Your love says, like an honest gentleman, and a courteous, and a kind, and a handsome, and I'll say a virtuous—where is your mother?[57]

JULIET: Where is my mother? She is inside the house! Where else would she be? What is this? "Your love says, like an honest gentleman . . . where is your mother?" Are you kidding me?!

NURSE: Why are you getting so angry? Goodness' sake, child! This is the reward I get for my aching bones? From now on, you handle your messages yourself!

JULIET: This isn't funny! Tell me! What says Romeo?!

NURSE: Do you have permission to go to confession today?

JULIET: Yes. So what?

---

[56] If you haven't figured it out yet, Nurse is being cruel to Juliet and having some fun at her expense by delaying the information Juliet craves and watching her get more and more flustered with each passing second that she has to wait.

[57] So cruel!

NURSE: Then go to Friar Lawrence's church. There, you will find a husband to make you a wife. Oh! Look at you now! Now you have some color in your cheeks! Go to the church now; Romeo is waiting for you there. I have to go somewhere else and pick up a rope ladder so your new husband can climb up to your room tonight after dark. I've done all the work so far, but at that point, it's all you—if you know what I mean! Go on. I'll go to dinner and let them know you've gone to confession. Go!

JULIET: Yes. Oh this is wonderful! I'll see you later!

They exit.

ACT 2, SCENE 6

Enter FRIAR LAWRENCE *and* ROMEO.

FRIAR LAWRENCE: I really hope Heaven smiles on us and what we are about to do, and we don't regret this later.

ROMEO: Agreed! But come on! What could possibly go wrong? It doesn't matter. No matter what happens, no matter how bad things could get, it can't counter the joy I have in seeing Juliet for even a minute. Honestly, once we are married, I can die a happy man![58]

FRIAR LAWRENCE: Just understand that although you are passionate now, the intensity will slow down. Love and passion can be like gunpowder kissing fire. A powerful explosion, for certain. But they can devour each other, and when that exploding passion is gone, there is nothing left. It is like your first bite of honey. At first it is sweet and wonderful, but if you eat the entire honeycomb in one sitting, the final bite will taste disgusting. But spread out, the honey will last a long time and always remain sweet to your taste. So my advice to you is to love moderately. Passion is a wonderful thing, but make sure that your love will last for the long haul.[59]

Enter JULIET.

And here comes the lady. She looks like she is floating across the floor! That is the look of love!

JULIET: Good evening, sir.

FRIAR LAWRENCE: Romeo shall welcome you for us both.

JULIET: And a thank you to both of you for all of this!

---

[58]   Foreshadowing, anyone?
[59]   Good advice.

ROMEO: Juliet, if you feel as much joy in this moment as me, say so. Proclaim it and let your words ring out like music in the air!

JULIET: My love, words cannot begin to describe my emotions right now. Just know that true love has grown to such a point that if it were money, I would not be able to add up even half of my wealth!

FRIAR LAWRENCE: Okay, okay, okay. Come with me. We'll make this quick, and I will absolutely not leave the two of you alone until after you are married. My heavens!

They exit.

END OF ACT 2

ACT 3

ACT 3, SCENE 1[60]

Enter MERCUTIO, BENVOLIO, *and their friends.*

BENVOLIO: Mercutio! I'm begging you, let's get out of here and go home! It's hot! And the Capulets are around and you know dang well if we meet them, we're gonna fight. Everybody seems angry right now! Let's go!

MERCUTIO: Dude, you're like one of those guys that goes into a bar, puts his sword on the table, and says, "God, I hope I don't have to use this!" And then after two drinks, you're using it to threaten the waiter for no reason!

BENVOLIO: Am I really like that?

MERCUTIO: Absolutely! You are the most hot-headed guy in Italy!

BENVOLIO: How so?

MERCUTIO: Man, if there were two of you, we would soon have none because you would kill each other! You would fight some dude because he has either one more or one less hair in his beard than you! You would fight someone for cracking nuts just because you have hazel eyes! You love fighting more than anyone I know! You fought a guy once because he coughed and woke up your dog! And remember when you got into a fight with that guy for wearing his new jacket before Easter? And that other clown you beat up for no other reason than he put old laces in his new shoes?![61] And you are going to talk to me about avoiding a fight? Right.

Enter TYBALT, PETRUCHIO, *and others.*

BENVOLIO: Oh man. By my head, here come the Capulets.

MERCUTIO: By my heel, I care not.

TYBALT *(to his companions)*: Follow my lead. I'll do the talking. *(to Mercutio, Benvolio, and the others)* Gentlemen, good evening. Can I have a word with one of you?

MERCUTIO: Just one word with one of us? Why not combine it with something? Make it a word and a fight!

---

60   As we begin act 3, know that the wedding ceremony has taken place offstage and, at this point, Romeo and Juliet are officially married.

61   Benvolio seems to take his fashion very seriously.

TYBALT: Oh trust me, I'll be up for that if you give me a reason.

MERCUTIO: Please, why don't YOU give ME a reason to beat you down? Bring it on!

TYBALT: Mercutio, you associate with Romeo!

MERCUTIO: So? Maybe we're in a band! Here's my instrument! *(draws sword)* Now let's dance, boy!

BENVOLIO: Guys! Chill out! We're in a public place! Let's go somewhere private and figure it out or we need to leave. People are watching![62]

MERCUTIO: So what? Let them watch. I'm not moving.[63]

Enter ROMEO.

TYBALT: Well, peace be with you, sir. Here comes my man.

MERCUTIO: I'll be damned before Romeo is ever your man.

TYBALT *(to Romeo)*: Romeo. The nicest word I have to call you is this: you are a villain![64]

ROMEO: Tybalt, normally, them would be fightin' words, but I now have a reason to love you so I'll let that pass. I am not a villain. So, farewell. You don't know me.

TYBALT: Boy, this will not excuse the offenses you've committed against me and my family! Turn and fight me!

ROMEO: Tybalt! I won't fight you! I didn't do anything to offend you or your family! I swear! Actually, I love you more than you know! I can't tell you the reason, but believe me! I love your name, good Capulet, as much as my own! Please be satisfied!

MERCUTIO: O calm, dishonorable, vile submission! Tybalt, you pussycat!

---

62   Remember the Prince's declaration from act 1: if they are caught fighting in the streets of Verona, they will be executed.

63   Why doesn't Mercutio seem worried about the law? Remember Mercutio is not a Montague or a Capulet. He is of the Royal Family, the Prince's cousin. He knows the Prince is not going to execute his cousin. And, in Mercutio's mind, he is not fighting because of the feud; he is simply defending his friend Romeo and therefore not breaking the law.

64   Oooo, no he didn't!

I'll fight you! Let's go!⁶⁵

TYBALT: What do you want from me?

MERCUTIO: Just one of your nine lives, Pussycat! You gonna draw your sword? 'Cos Imma bout to cut you!

TYBALT: Bring it.

He draws his sword.

ROMEO: Mercutio, NO! Stop! Put your sword away!

MERCUTIO *(to Tybalt)*: Let's dance.

MERCUTIO *and* TYBALT *fight.*⁶⁶

ROMEO: Benvolio! Help me break this up! Guys, stop it! Tybalt! Mercutio! Stop! The Prince forbids fighting! Stop! Hold up! Mercutio! No!⁶⁷

TYBALT *stabs* MERCUTIO.

PETRUCHIO: *(seeing what Tybalt has done)* Tybalt! We gotta go man! Now!

TYBALT, PETRUCHIO, *and their posse exit.*

MERCUTIO: Dang it! I'm hurt. Dang your families and your goddang feud! Did he get anything? Did I hit him at all?

BENVOLIO: You hurt, man?

---

65 Mercutio is shocked and disgusted by Romeo's submission and unwillingness to fight Tybalt. He decides to defend his friend who refuses to defend himself. FYI: Mercutio starts referring to Tybalt as a cat because Tybalt is the name of a cat in an old folktale that they all would know.

66 With both these guys coming from powerful families, they've both been trained and this fight should be pretty good—choreographer needed!

67 Because of their extensive training, their dueling was most likely controlled and neither was in any real danger, other than some possible cuts. Neither has any real desire to kill the other, despite their big talk. Neither of them have anything to gain with the other's death. Tybalt certainly doesn't want to kill a member of the Royal Family, but can't back down from a challenge. Mercutio is defending his friend's honor; but while he could avoid the punishment for fighting, he knows he couldn't avoid the punishment for murder. This is about machismo and testosterone more than anything else. However, things go off the rails because Romeo now jumps between them which upsets the timing and precision and, most importantly, their line of sight. Because of this, Tybalt (accidentally) stabs Mercutio under Romeo's arm. Not good.

MERCUTIO: Yeah, but it's just a scratch. Yeah . . . a scratch. But it's enough. Someone needs to get me a doctor.

ROMEO: It can't be that bad . . . can it?

MERCUTIO: Well, it's not as deep as a well or wide as a church door, but trust me: it's enough. If you look for me tomorrow, you'll find me a GRAVE man![68] No . . . I'm dying. God DAMN both your families! How did he get me?! How could HE beat ME?! He's a clown! A pussycat! Romeo, why the heck did you get between us? I had it under control; I was hurt under your arm.

ROMEO: I thought it was for the best . . . .

MERCUTIO: Benvolio, help me to some house. I'm about to drop. Damn both your houses! A plague on both your houses! You've made worm's meat of me! This is it. GOD DAMN you all![69]

All but ROMEO *exit.*

ROMEO: Mercutio . . . the Prince's cousin . . . my friend . . . is dying for defending me . . . from Tybalt who was disrespecting me. Tybalt . . . who has been my cousin for an hour. Oh Juliet. Your beauty made me soft!

Enter BENVOLIO.

BENVOLIO: Romeo. Mercutio is dead.

ROMEO: This black day is going to lead to something. This ain't over.

Enter TYBALT.[70]

BENVOLIO: Tybalt is back!

ROMEO: Alive in triumph and Mercutio dead! Mercy be damned. Fire-eyed fury be my conduct now! *(to Tybalt)* Tybalt! Take back what you said earlier! Mercutio's soul is just a little above our heads waiting for YOU to keep him company. Either you or me, but one of us must go with him!

TYBALT: You, wretched boy, will go with him!

---

68   Even dying, he manages a terrible pun. Gotta love this guy!
69   Imagine these were the final words your best friend said to you before he died. Imagine your best friend received his fatal wound because you got in the way. Imagine your best friend died defending you because you wouldn't defend yourself. Now, imagine your best friend asking someone else to help him and leaving you alone to think about what you did . . . and didn't do . . . to stew in your thoughts.
70   Why he came back is anybody's guess . . . is it to gloat in victory? Is it to see if Mercutio is okay? We don't know.

ROMEO: Let's find out.

They fight.[71]

TYBALT *dies.*

BENVOLIO: Romeo get out of here! The Citizens are coming! Tybalt's dead! Don't just stand there! If you are taken in, the Prince will execute you! Go!

ROMEO: Oh, I am Fortune's fool!

BENVOLIO: Why are you still here?!

ROMEO *exits.*

Enter CITIZENS.

CITIZEN: Where is Tybalt? The killer of Mercutio! Where did he go?

BENVOLIO: He's right there.

CITIZEN: Get up, Tybalt! I charge you in the Prince's name with murder! Get up![72]

Enter PRINCE, MONTAGUE, CAPULET, *their wives, and all.*

PRINCE: Where are the men who started this fight?

BENVOLIO: Prince, I can tell you everything. Over there lies Tybalt, who was killed by Romeo. Tybalt killed your cousin, Mercutio, and so Romeo then killed him.

LADY CAPULET: Tybalt! My nephew! Oh Prince! Blood is spilled from my family! Prince, if you are true, for blood of ours, shed blood of Montague!

PRINCE: Benvolio, what happened here?

BENVOLIO: Okay. Well, Tybalt showed up looking to fight Romeo, but Romeo didn't want to fight. Romeo actually was really calm and respectful and humble; he talked about how fights are met with your royal displeasure. But no matter what Romeo said, Tybalt wouldn't listen and kept pushing. Then Mercutio stepped in to fight Tybalt and defend Romeo. They fought a helluva fight. It was pretty awesome actually. But then Romeo jumped in and tried to break it up. Under Romeo's arm, Tybalt struck Mercutio. And that was the hit

---

71   While both are skilled fighters, Tybalt is a bit off his game knowing that with Mercutio's death he may be facing execution, and Romeo is fighting with a fury and passion that is unmatched by his foe. He fights for his friend. Ultimately, Romeo triumphs.

72   Sorry Citizen . . . he ain't getting up from this.

that killed him. Tybalt ran away. But then he came back again. At that point, Romeo was triggered and angry and they went at it fast. Before I could do anything, Romeo killed Tybalt and then he ran off. I swear to God this is the truth.

LADY CAPULET: He is a Montague! He's protecting his family! He's lying to make Tybalt look like the villain! There must have been twenty of them all ganging up on Tybalt! I beg for justice, which you, Prince, must give! Romeo killed Tybalt: Romeo must not live!

PRINCE: Romeo killed him; he killed Mercutio. Who pays the price for the death of MY cousin?

MONTAGUE: Not Romeo, Prince; he was Mercutio's friend. He simply did what you would have done anyway: executed the murderer of your cousin. That is where it should end: with the life of Tybalt.

PRINCE: And for that offense, we immediately exile Romeo from Verona. I am now involved in your feud. My cousin is dead and bleeding because of it. I will now punish you so that you ALL repent the loss of my family. I will be deaf to pleading and excuses. I will ignore prayers. And don't you dare try to bribe me. Don't bother with any of it. Let Romeo leave now. We will not follow or search for him. But if he ever shows his face here again, that hour will be his last.

They exit with Capulet's men carrying off Tybalt's body.

ACT 3, SCENE 2

Enter JULIET.[73]

JULIET: Come on night! I am so sick of daytime right now. Night needs to get here! You know why? Because when night comes, so does Romeo! We're married, but have yet to consummate our marriage . . . I want to lose my virginity! I'm so excited for him to come here. I'm like a little kid that gets new clothes but isn't allowed to wear them!

Enter NURSE.[74]

Here comes the nurse! Oh I hope she says stuff about Romeo! Oooo, is that the ladder Romeo is to use to climb up to my room tonight?

NURSE: Uh, yeah, the ladder . . . .

JULIET: Nurse . . . what's wrong?

---

73   Juliet has no idea what just happened.
74   Nurse DOES know what just happened and is obviously distraught.

NURSE: OH MY GOD, HE IS DEAD! What a terrible day! He's dead and we're screwed!

JULIET: What?! What are you talking about?

NURSE: Romeo! Who would have ever thought it? Oh Romeo!

JULIET: What in the hell are you saying?! Did Romeo kill himself? Is Romeo dead? Just say yes if he is dead and no if he isn't. One simple word will tell me if I am happy or sad.

NURSE: I saw the wound. I saw the blood. I saw the corpse. I fainted at the sight of the gore.

JULIET: My heart is broken. My world is over. This is too much.

NURSE: OH TYBALT! I never thought I would live to see you dead!

JULIET: Wait, what? Are both Romeo AND Tybalt dead? Who is living if those two are dead?

NURSE: Tybalt is dead and Romeo is banished for killing him.

JULIET: Romeo killed Tybalt?

NURSE: Yes.

JULIET: How could someone look so beautiful and yet be so vile? He has the heart of a snake, but it is hidden by his beautiful face! Oh, that deceit should live in such a gorgeous palace!

NURSE: Yes! Men suck! Shame on Romeo!

JULIET: How dare you say something bad about Romeo! Shame on you! And shame on me for saying such terrible things about my love!

NURSE: Wait . . . what? You're going to speak nicely about the guy that murdered your cousin?

JULIET: He is my husband and I will not speak badly of him. Think about it. Why would Romeo kill my cousin? Because my butthole cousin probably tried to kill him first. Romeo is alive and Tybalt, who would have killed him, is dead. This is good![75] So why am I still crying? You said something that is striking me to my heart. You said Romeo is banished. That is way worse than Tybalt's death. Saying he is banished is like telling me that Tybalt, my parents, myself, and Romeo are all dead. There are no words to describe the pain that word gives me. Where are my parents?

---

75   Juliet is pretty perceptive here. She knows her cousin well.

NURSE: Crying over Tybalt. Did you want me to take you to them?

JULIET: No. By the time they are done crying over him, I will still be crying over Romeo. Just take away this rope ladder. Poor ladder. You were supposed to be Romeo's path to my bed. Instead, I am going to die a virgin. Death will take my virginity now.

NURSE: No. I know where Romeo is. He is in Friar Lawrence's room. I will get him and bring him to you!

JULIET: Oh yay! Please find him and give him this ring. Tell him he needs to come here and give me a proper farewell!

They exit.

ACT 3, SCENE 3

Enter FRIAR LAWRENCE.

FRIAR LAWRENCE: Romeo! Get out here. You are the unluckiest man I know.

Enter ROMEO.

ROMEO: Father, what news? What is the Prince's judgment?

FRIAR LAWRENCE: He decided not to have you executed. Rather, you are now banished from Verona.

ROMEO: NO! Please don't say that! Banishment is way worse than death!

FRIAR LAWRENCE: You are just banished from Verona. The world is really big!

ROMEO: No! You're wrong! Verona IS the world. So to say I am banished from Verona is the same as saying I am banished from the world, and being banished from the world is the same as being dead!

FRIAR LAWRENCE: Ungrateful little boy! The punishment for what you did is supposed to be execution. The Prince changed it to banishment for you. This is mercy, and you don't see it!

ROMEO: No. This is torture, not mercy. Juliet is my world and she is here in Verona. Dogs and cats and even little bugs can look at her whenever they want, but me? I won't be able to see her ever again. Knowing she is alive and not being able to see her is the worst thing I can think of. I would rather be dead.

FRIAR LAWRENCE: Just listen to me. Let me give you advice.

ROMEO: NO! You don't understand! You can't possibly understand what I'm going through! Were you as young as me, had Juliet as your love, were married for an hour, had killed Tybalt, and, like me, were banished, then you could talk! Then you would pull out your hair and fall to the ground and cry like am doing right now![76] *(falls to the ground and cries)*

(knocking at the door)

FRIAR LAWRENCE: Crap! Someone's here. Romeo, go hide!

ROMEO: No. I will hide in my own groans and sighs.

FRIAR LAWRENCE: I'll be right there! —Romeo, get up! They'll take you!

(knock)

Coming! —This is so stupid. —Romeo, go to my study and hide!

(knock)

Who is it?

NURSE: I come from Juliet. Let me in.

FRIAR LAWRENCE *opens the door.* NURSE *enters.*

FRIAR LAWRENCE: Welcome.

NURSE: Where's Romeo?

FRIAR LAWRENCE: There on the floor, drunk on his own tears.

NURSE: Good Lord. He's acting just like Juliet, weeping and blubbering. Romeo, GET UP! Be a man!

ROMEO: Nurse, how is Juliet? What does she say about this whole situation?

NURSE: Well, she doesn't really say much, she just cries a lot. She cries out "Tybalt!" and then "Romeo!"

ROMEO: That name! My name! I hate it! *(draws a dagger)* Friar, show me where my name is on my body so I can cut it out!

FRIAR LAWRENCE: Enough! Put the dagger down. I am so done with this! Are you a man? You look like one, but you're acting like a little girl. You amaze me! I thought you would be in a better mindset right now. Are you really going to kill yourself right now? How do you think that will that affect Juliet? Huh? Oh you didn't think of her? Too busy thinking about yourself? Shame on you! You are making a mockery of your wedding vows! You're like a stupid

---

76   And the immaturity is showing itself again!

soldier who shoots himself in the foot with his own weapon! Rise up! Juliet is alive! That should make you happy! Tybalt wanted to kill you, but you killed him instead. That should make you happy! The law threatened death, but was changed to exile. That should make you happy! A pack of blessings are following you around and happiness is raining down on you, but like a misbehaved, sullen wench, you just pout and cry and wallow in your own self-pity. Get up! Go! Go to your wife's chamber and comfort her tonight. Then, either before the guards are set tonight or right after the guards leave in the morning, go to our neighboring town of Mantua where you will live until we can make your marriage public, regroup your friends, ask the Prince for forgiveness, and bring you back with a ton more joy than this sadness with which you are now leaving. —Nurse. Go there first and get the family to go to bed, which shouldn't be too hard since they've been grieving all day. Romeo is coming!

NURSE: Wow. Man can give a speech! I'm on my way. Here, Romeo. This is a ring that Juliet told me to give to you.

ROMEO: Okay! I'm feeling better now!

FRIAR LAWRENCE: Get out of here! I'll send word to you in Mantua of any news that happens here. Give me your hand. Farewell.

ROMEO: Thank you! Farewell.

They exit.

ACT 3, SCENE 4

Enter CAPULET, LADY CAPULET, *and* PARIS.[77]

CAPULET: I'm sorry sir, but we haven't had time to really talk to our daughter about your marriage. Juliet loved Tybalt dearly, and so did I. It's very late and she will not come down tonight. If it wasn't for the fact that you are here, I would have gone to bed awhile ago.

PARIS: I understand. It's hard to be romantic at a time like this. Send my love to your daughter.

LADY CAPULET: I will. I will talk to her in the morning and get her decision on the marriage. Tonight she is too sad.

CAPULET: Hold on. I am going to speak for her. I have no doubt that she will respect my decision. Wife, go and talk to Juliet and tell her of Paris's love and this Wednesday . . . wait, what day is it?

PARIS: Monday.

---

77   Remember him?

CAPULET: Monday! Haha! Well, Wednesday is too soon. Let's say Thursday. Wife, tell Juliet that on Thursday she shall be married to this noble young man! Paris, will you be ready by then? Is this too fast? It won't be a huge wedding; just a few guests, because if we celebrate too much, it may look like we didn't care about Tybalt. What do you say to Thursday?

PARIS: My Lord, I wish Thursday were tomorrow!

CAPULET: Excellent! Thursday it is! Wife, go tell Juliet the wonderful news! Let's go prepare for a wedding![78]

They exit.

ACT 3, SCENE 5[79]

JULIET: Are you leaving? It's not time yet! It's still night. That bird singing outside is a nightingale, not the lark. I promise!

ROMEO: No. It was the lark. A morning bird. I wish you were right. But look out the window. You can see the streaks of morning coming up over the mountain. There are no stars in the sky. I must leave and live, or stay and die.

JULIET: No. Those streaks of light are not daylight. They are meteors to light your way to Mantua! So, you see? You don't need to leave yet!

ROMEO: Fine. You win! You're right! That isn't the sun and that bird is totally a nightingale! I want to stay! Let me be taken and put to death! Who cares! Let's just lay around and talk. It's not daytime!

JULIET: No. It is day. You have to go. It is the lark singing outside my window. I hate that bird so much right now. It's getting lighter and lighter outside.

ROMEO: The lighter it gets outside, the darker my heart feels inside.

Enter NURSE.

NURSE: Madam.

JULIET: Nurse?

NURSE: Your mother is on her way up! It's day!

NURSE *exits.*

JULIET: Then, window, let daylight in, and let my life out.

---

78   Uh-oh.

79   It is early morning, and Romeo and Juliet are lying in bed. They have consummated their marriage . . . in other words, neither of them is a virgin anymore.

ROMEO *climbs out the window.*

ROMEO: Farewell, my love. Give me one last kiss before I climb down.

They kiss and ROMEO *descends.*

JULIET: And so you leave. My love, my lord, my husband, my friend. You must contact me whenever you get the chance! Oh God, how long will it be before I can see you again?

ROMEO: Farewell. I will never miss any opportunity to send you my love.

JULIET: Do you think we will ever see each other again?

ROMEO: Without a doubt. Years from now, this will all just be a part of our love story!

JULIET: My God. I have a bad feeling in my soul. Now that you are so far below me, it looks to me like you are dead in the bottom of a tomb. You look pale.

ROMEO: Trust me, so do you. Sorrow is sucking the blood from us. Goodbye, farewell, adieu . . . .

ROMEO *exits.*

JULIET: Please Fate, be fickle and bring him back to me soon.

Enter LADY CAPULET.

LADY CAPULET: Daughter, are you up?

JULIET: *(at the window) (aside)* Mother? Why is she in my room this early? What does she want?

LADY CAPULET: How are you, Juliet?

JULIET: Madam, I am not well.

LADY CAPULET: Still crying over your cousin's death? Why? Are you going to bring him back with your tears? Sorry, you can't. He's dead. Be done with this. Some grief shows love, but too much grief shows a lack of intelligence and maturity. So get over it.[80]

JULIET: Can't you just let me cry? This hurts!

LADY CAPULET: Well, I don't think you're crying so much for your cousin as much as the fact that the villain who killed him is still alive!

JULIET: What villain is that?

---

80   Wow! This woman is cold! He just died yesterday!

LADY CAPULET: That Romeo!

JULIET: Yeah. Romeo. He's the one who makes my heart hurt.[81]

LADY CAPULET: Of course! That murderer is still alive!

JULIET: Right. I wish I could get my hands on him so I could repay him for what he has done!

LADY CAPULET: Oh, don't you worry my dear. We will have our vengeance. I'm going to send someone to Mantua, where that little bastard lives, and slip him some poison so he will soon keep Tybalt company. Then, I hope you will be satisfied.

JULIET: I won't be satisfied until I see him . . . dead . . . my heart is dead for my lost family. If you find a man willing to bring it to Romeo, I want to be the one to make the poison. That way I can make sure it is done right. Then when Romeo drinks it, he will soon sleep quietly. Oh, how I hate to hear his name and not go to him and bring all the love I have for my family down upon him![82]

LADY CAPULET: We can make that happen, my dear. But now, on to other matters. I have great news!

JULIET: Great news would be welcome on a day like this. What is it?

LADY CAPULET: Well, your father loves you so much that in order to end your grief, he has arranged a day of joy for you! It was all so unexpected!

JULIET: This sounds wonderful! What is it?

LADY CAPULET: You're getting married on Thursday morning! The gallant, young, and noble gentleman Count Paris will make you a joyful bride!

JULIET: What?! No! He will absolutely NOT make me a joyful bride! What in the world, Mom?! Why is this happening so fast? He hasn't even asked me out! We've barely spoken! Now I have to marry him? No. You can go and tell

---

81   From here until the end of this portion of the conversation, Juliet's lines all have a double meaning. She is saying things in a way that reflects her true feelings but will not arouse any sort of suspicion from her mother.

82   Did you get all that? Her mom thinks she is saying that she wants to see him dead and be the one who makes the poison that kills him to bring vengeance on him. Whereas she is saying she wants to see him and that her heart is dead for lost family—Romeo is her family now!—and that she wants to mix the poison so that it won't kill him, but simply put him to sleep, sabotaging the murder attempt. Oh, and also to bring her love to him. This is a cute exchange where we can see the cool tricks of language to create the meaning we want! Read the original text to see how Shakespeare accomplishes the same thing (act 3, scene 5, lines 98–107)!

my father that I will not marry yet, and if I did, I would rather marry Romeo . . . uh, I mean . . . who you know I hate, rather than Paris![83] Good news, my butt!

LADY CAPULET: Here he comes. You can tell him yourself and see how he takes it.

Enter CAPULET *and* NURSE.

CAPULET: Are you still crying, my girl? Wow! How can such a small body produce so many tears? Well my wife? Did you tell her the news?

LADY CAPULET: Yes, sir, but she said no. She gives you thanks. She may as well get married to her grave.

CAPULET: What? Are you serious? She said no? She isn't grateful? She isn't proud? She doesn't consider herself blessed that we found such a worthy gentleman to be her groom?

JULIET: I am thankful for your love and I appreciate what you are trying to do, but I cannot be proud to marry someone I hate!

CAPULET: What? How? Huh? What is this? "Proud" and "thankful," and yet NOT thankful and NOT proud? Let me explain something to you: you do not thank me and show me no pride, but you better get your prissy little butt to that church on Thursday or I will drag you there myself, you good-for-nothing little twit!

LADY CAPULET: Calm down, my lord!

JULIET: *(kneeling)* Good father, I'm begging you on my knees. Just listen to me for a minute!

CAPULET: Shut up you disobedient wretch! I tell you what: You get to that church on Thursday or never look me in the face. Don't ever speak to me again. Don't say a word. It's taking all my control not to beat the hell out of you! Wife—we thought we were blessed to have this one and only child. She was our gift from God. But now I see she is one child too many and that she is actually a curse and we would be better off childless.

NURSE: My God in Heaven, you can't say such things to her!

CAPULET: Oh, shut up! Go gossip with your friends somewhere else!

NURSE: I've never gossiped!

CAPULET: Get out!

---

83   Oops!

NURSE: May I not speak?

CAPULET: Just be quiet you mumbling fool! Nobody wants to hear your opinion!

LADY CAPULET: You need to calm down.

CAPULET: It makes me mad! Day and night, work and play, alone and in company, I have busted my butt trying to find her a proper match for a husband. And now I have provided a gentleman of noble birth, good property, youth—a member of the ROYAL FAMILY. He is as honorable as they come. Everything anyone would ever want in a man! And to hear this little wretched, whining fool answer with "I won't get married! I can't love! I'm too young! I don't like him! Please pardon me!" Oh . . . I'll pardon you. You can find somewhere else to sleep, because you won't be living in my house. Think about that. I am not joking. Thursday is near. Take this to heart: You are mine. And I will give you to my friend. And if you refuse? Hang, beg, starve, die in the streets, for by my soul, I'll never acknowledge you as mine. Nothing I have will ever do you any good. You will be dead to me. Trust me. Think seriously about your choices. This is a promise and I will not change my mind![84]

LORD CAPULET *exits.*

JULIET: Why is Fate doing this to me? Is there no pity? Mom! My sweet mother! Please help me. Delay this marriage for a month, or even just a week. Or, if you don't, you might as well make my wedding bed in the tomb where Tybalt's body lies!

LADY CAPULET: Don't talk to me. I won't speak a word. Do what you will,

---

[84]   I'm often asked how Lord Capulet went from the man in act 1, who told Paris that he had to win her consent and seemed so loving, to this angry, threatening man here in act 3. The answer has to do with the situation. I don't think it ever really occurred to him that she may say no, even back in act 1. But more pressing than that is the position he has now put himself in. He just told Paris that he could marry Juliet and had no doubt she would respect his decision. And now she said no. What is he supposed to do? Go back to Paris and say nevermind!? How would that reflect on him and his family name? To reject a member of the Royal Family? It would look like he had no control over his daughter and that would be unacceptable. Also remember that back in this era, marriage (especially in the elite circles) was as much about politics as anything else. This marriage was not just about Juliet; this marriage was about uniting the Capulet family with the Royal Family. Therefore, it would increase Lord Capulet's power and influence. At this point, telling Paris no is not possible in Capulet's mind and if Juliet does not follow through with the marriage, Capulet will lose standing in Verona and lose any chance he has at that power and influence forever. That is why he reacts this way; he NEEDS this wedding to happen.

but I am done with you.[85]

LADY CAPULET *exits.*

JULIET: Oh God! Nurse! How do we stop this? I'm already married! I vowed to stay true to Romeo until "death do us part!" He is still alive! I can't be married to two men! Nurse, comfort me! Help me! What should I do?

NURSE: Okay . . . here it is. Romeo is banished. He is not coming back. If he does, it must be in secret. Given the situation, I think it would be best if you married Paris. He really is a lovely gentleman! Honestly, Romeo is a dishrag compared to him. I know this is not what you want to hear right now, but in truth, I think you will be very happy in this second marriage, for it actually excels your first. And even if it didn't, your first husband is dead or at least as good as dead with you living here and of no use to him.

JULIET: Is this how you really feel? From your heart?

NURSE: From my soul too.

JULIET: Okay.

NURSE: What?

JULIET: You've comforted me and you make a lot of sense. Go tell my mother that I have gone to Friar Lawrence for confession, for having displeased my father.

NURSE: I will. And this is a good choice.

NURSE *exits.*

JULIET: Dang old woman. Wicked fiend! So she thinks it is better for me to break my marriage vows to Romeo after praising him so many times! Fine. Leave, "friend." You and my heart are forever split from now on. I'll go to the friar to see how we can fix this, and if all else fails, I know I have the power to take my own life.

JULIET *exits.*

END OF ACT 3

---

85   Cold!

ACT 4

ACT 4, SCENE 1

Enter FRIAR LAWRENCE *and* COUNT PARIS.

FRIAR LAWRENCE: On Thursday, sir? That's really fast!

PARIS: It is what Lord Capulet wants, and I am fine with it!

FRIAR LAWRENCE: You say you don't know how the lady feels about it? This doesn't seem right. I don't like it.

PARIS: She can't stop crying over Tybalt's death, so I have not been able to court her properly. But it is because of this extreme grief that her father, in his wisdom, wants to have this marriage done quickly. He feels that she is falling too far into despair and that it is becoming dangerous for her. His hope is that this wedding will stop her tears and bring her happiness back. Now you know why it must be done quickly.

FRIAR LAWRENCE: *(aside)* And I wish I could give a reason to delay it! *(to Paris)* Look, sir, here comes the lady toward us!

Enter JULIET.

PARIS: Good morning, my lady and my wife!

JULIET: I'm not your wife yet.

PARIS: Yes, well, you will be on Thursday!

JULIET: It is what it is.

FRIAR LAWRENCE: Truth.

PARIS: Umm . . . okay . . . uh . . . so . . . are you here for confession?

JULIET: If I answer that, then I would be confessing to you.

PARIS: Well, I hope that you confess to him that you love me!

JULIET: I will confess to you that I love him.

PARIS: Okay. Sure, but you do love me . . . right?

JULIET: If I do, it will be worth more if I confess it behind your back than to your face. So I'll just stay quiet on that subject while you are here.

PARIS: My dear, your tears have abused your face. You don't look pretty after all this crying.[86]

JULIET: Oh, it's not the tears' fault. My face was ugly even before I started crying.

PARIS: What?! No, that's not true. Don't insult yourself like that!

JULIET: It's not an insult if it is true. And besides, I said it to my own face rather than behind my back, so it is okay.

PARIS: Your face is mine now, and you have insulted it!

JULIET: Fine. Whatever. It's yours. It certainly isn't mine. *(to Friar Lawrence)* Father, are you available now or shall I come back at another time?

FRIAR LAWRENCE: I am available now, daughter. *(to Paris)* Sir, I must ask for privacy now for the sake of the lady.

PARIS: Oh God forbid I disturb her devotion! Juliet, I will see you on Thursday morning. Until then, adieu, and keep this holy kiss.

PARIS *kisses* JULIET *and then exits.*

JULIET: Oh, shut the door! And after you do that, come cry with me! I am without hope!

FRIAR LAWRENCE: Oh Juliet, I already heard everything and I am at my wit's end. I heard that you are going to be marrying that guy on Thursday!

JULIET: Don't tell me you heard all about it, unless you can tell me how we can prevent it! If you can't find a way to help me, I will use this knife and help myself! *(She pulls out a knife.)* God joined my heart to Romeo's and you joined our hands in marriage. And I will die before my hand is joined to another man's! So give me a solution. Give me a plan as to how we fix this, or I will stab myself in my heart and die right here, right now! Don't just stand there silent! Say something! If you can't give me a remedy for this situation, then I WANT to die!

FRIAR LAWRENCE: Now just hold on. I think I may have a plan. It's desperate, but it could work. If you are willing to die rather than marry Paris, then it is likely that you would be willing to undertake something LIKE death to get out of this. If you are willing to do something risky and dangerous to avoid this shame, then I think I can help you.

JULIET: Are you seriously asking this question? Do you know what I would rather do than marry Paris? I would rather jump off the walls of any tower! I

---

86   Oh ... he's smooth, isn't he?

would walk through the dark, crime-filled alleys of the city! I would walk into a cave filled with snakes! I would be chained to roaring bears! I would spend every night in a dead man's tomb lying on the slab of stone next to the corpse under his shroud! I would do any of these things rather than marry Paris! Do you doubt me?

FRIAR LAWRENCE: Okay, I get it. Jeez. Here is the plan: Go home. Be happy. Agree to marry Paris. Tomorrow is Wednesday. So tomorrow night, make sure you go to bed alone. Don't even let the Nurse sleep in your room. *(He holds out a vial of liquid.)* Take this vial, while lying in bed, and drink it. All of it. When you do, all of your veins will stop pumping blood and you will have no pulse. You will become cold and you will have no breath from your lips. The color in your cheeks and lips will fade to an ash gray and your eyes will look empty. You will be stiff, stark and cold, and you will look dead in every regard.[87] This deathlike state will last for forty-two hours. And then you will wake up as if from a pleasant sleep. Now, on Thursday morning, when you are to be awakened from sleep, you will be found "dead." Then, as is the custom in this country, you will be dressed in your finest clothes and taken to the Capulet tomb, where all your ancestors are buried. In the meantime, before you wake up, I will write a letter to Romeo letting him know the details of this plan. He will be instructed to sneak back into Verona, and then he and I will be in the tomb when you wake up. Then, that same night, you and Romeo will head back to Mantua and live happily ever after while avoiding the shame of either being married to two men or being ostracized by your father. This should work so long as you don't get too scared to follow through with it.

JULIET: Give me the vial. Don't talk to me about fear.

FRIAR LAWRENCE: *(handing JULIET the vial)* Here. Now go. Be strong and fearless. I'll send the fastest friar I can find to Mantua with a letter for Romeo.

JULIET: Lord give me strength! Farewell, dear Father.

They exit in different directions.

ACT 4, SCENE 2

Enter CAPULET, LADY CAPULET, NURSE, and two or three servingmen.

CAPULET: Go and invite the people that are on this list.

One or two of the servingmen exit with Capulet's list.

---

[87] See? I told you that his expertise in medicine and herbs would come into play!

You! Go hire twenty cooks for the reception.

SERVINGMAN: Oh I will find the best of the best sir! I will ask if they can lick their fingers!

CAPULET: Excuse me? Why would you ask them that? That's just weird.

SERVINGMAN: Oh my good sir, only a bad cook is unwilling to lick his fingers! Good cooks love to taste test their creations! Therefore, if a cook refuses to lick his own fingers, then he is not good enough for you!

CAPULET: Whatever. Just go.

SERVINGMAN *exits.*

We're never going to pull this off . . . where is my daughter? Did she go to Friar Lawrence?

NURSE: Yes.

CAPULET: Good. Maybe he can talk some sense into the obstinate, selfish little wench.

Enter JULIET.

NURSE: Oooo, here she comes from confession, and she looks happy!

CAPULET: How are you now my stubborn girl? Where have you been?

JULIET: Where I learned to repent the sin of being disobedient and opposing you and your will. Holy Friar Lawrence has advised me to beg your pardon. *(falling to her knees)* So my dear father, I ask you to please forgive me. From now on, I will always be ruled by you.

CAPULET: Someone go get Count Paris! Tell him of this! We'll do the wedding tomorrow morning![88]

JULIET: I met the young lord when I was with Friar Lawrence. I showed him all the love I could while still maintaining my modesty.[89]

CAPULET: Well I'm glad! This is fantastic! Stand up. *(*JULIET *rises)* This is how it is supposed to be. Seriously. Someone go get the count! Now I thank God for this friar! The whole city, and this family especially, is indebted to him!

JULIET: Nurse, will you come with me and help me find a nice dress and jewelry to wear at the ceremony tomorrow?

---

88   Uh-oh . . . monkey wrench in the plan.
89   Sure she did. I'm not sure I would call that "love."

LADY CAPULET: No. Everybody just hold on a second! Not until Thursday! We don't have enough time to get everything set by tomorrow!

CAPULET: Go, Nurse. Go with her. We are going to the church tomorrow.

JULIET *and the* NURSE *exit.*

LADY CAPULET: We won't get things done in time. It's already getting late!

CAPULET: Oh hush, woman! I will stay up and get it done. It will be lovely. I think you should go help Juliet. Help her find the best attire for the event. I won't go to bed tonight. Let me do this. I will do the "housewife" stuff this once. Everyone is working so hard! I'll go talk to Count Paris myself and prepare him for tomorrow. My heart is light in my chest since my wayward girl has come back to her senses and to us!

They exit.

ACT 4, SCENE 3

Enter JULIET *and* NURSE.

JULIET: Yes, this dress is the best. But gentle Nurse, I ask that you leave me alone tonight. I have a lot of praying to do. You know that my situation is filled with sin and I have to repent and beg that heaven will still smile on me.

Enter LADY CAPULET.

LADY CAPULET: Are you busy? Do you need my help?

JULIET: No, Madam, we have chosen everything we need for tomorrow. So, I ask that you leave me alone and let the Nurse stay with you tonight. I am sure you could use any help that is available because of the suddenness of the ceremony.

LADY CAPULET: Good night. Go to bed. You have a big day tomorrow!

LADY CAPULET *and* NURSE *exit.*

JULIET: Farewell—God knows when we shall meet again.[90] I feel so cold . . . a chill is in me. I'm . . . scared. I want them back so they can comfort me!

---

90   This always makes me sad. She is saying farewell to her mother and the woman who was, for all intents and purposes, a second mother. A final farewell. She knows that she will never see them again. Ever. They only think they are saying good night. They don't know it is goodbye.

Nurse! —No. Stop it. What could she do here? I need to take this next step myself. Come here vial. *(She takes out the vial.)* What if this potion doesn't work at all? Will I have to get married tomorrow morning? *(She takes out her knife and puts it down beside her.)* Nope. This will solve that issue.

But what if it is actually poison that the friar gave me so that I would be dead and then he wouldn't be dishonored for marrying me to two men? Could it be? No. He is still a friar and a good and holy man. And last time I checked, murder is still a pretty big sin.

What if I wake up before Romeo gets there? The wedding was moved up a day after all. There's a scary thought. Would I suffocate in the tomb? Would Romeo come to find a dead Juliet?

And even if I do live, and I wake up . . . alone . . . in the dark . . . in a tomb . . . surrounded by the dead bodies and skulls and bones of hundreds of years of dead Capulets, including Tybalt who is still gonna be festering in his shroud. And ghosts! I've heard there are ghosts and spirits in these graveyards! And the smell . . . oh God, the smell. If I wake up like this, I would surely go mad! I would probably start playing with my forefathers' bones! I would knock Tybalt off his table! I would take some old ancestor's bones and start bashing my brains in!

Oh look! I think I see the ghost of Tybalt looking for Romeo for vengeance! Stop Tybalt! Stop! Oh Romeo, Romeo, Romeo! Here's a drink and toast. I drink to you!

JULIET *drinks the potion and falls upon her bed.*

ACT 4, SCENE 4

Enter **LADY CAPULET** *and* **NURSE**.

LADY CAPULET: Nurse. Here, take these keys and get more spices.

NURSE: They are asking for dates and quinces in the kitchen.

Enter **CAPULET**.

CAPULET: Come on! Let's go! The rooster crowed for the second time and the curfew bell rang. That means it is after 3:00 a.m.! Angelica! Please go and get some meat pies. And get the good stuff! Spare no expense!

LADY CAPULET: Go to bed, you old maid! If you stay up all night, you will be sick tomorrow and miss the wedding!

CAPULET: You back off woman! I have stayed up all night for lesser reasons than this and I've never gotten sick!

LADY CAPULET: Uh-huh. Oh I know. You used to stay up all night chasing women! But I'll keep you from chasing anything or anybody now!

LADY CAPULET and **NURSE** exit.

CAPULET: Such a jealous woman!

Enter three or four servingmen with spits, logs, and baskets.

Hey! What have you got there?

FIRST SERVINGMAN: Things for the cook, but I have no idea what they are specifically.

CAPULET: Fine. Go to the kitchen. Faster!

FIRST SERVINGMAN exits.

You there! Go get drier logs. Call Peter; he can show you where they are.

SECOND SERVINGMAN: Sir, I don't need Peter to show me anything. I can figure it out without bothering him.

CAPULET: Sounds good! Then I will call you Mr. Loggerhead!

SECOND SERVINGMAN exits.

My God, it is almost day! The count will be here soon and he said he would be bringing the band for music!

Music starts playing.

Oh crap! I hear him coming! Nurse! Wife! Where are you two? Nurse!

Enter **NURSE**.

Nurse, go wake up Juliet. Get her dressed and all done up. I'll talk to Paris here for a few minutes to buy you some time. Hurry! Hurry! Paris is here! Hurry up, I said!

CAPULET exits.

ACT 4, SCENE 5

JULIET is in her bed. The **NURSE** enters and approaches the bed.

NURSE: Madam! Mistress! Juliet! Still asleep? It is time to get up! Come on you lazy girl! It's your wedding day! Oh well, I suppose you need your sleep because Count Paris won't give you any rest tonight! Haha! God forgive me! Are you still asleep? Goodness, child! I'll wake you up! Madam! Madam! MADAM! Maybe I should let the count come wake you! He'll get you up!

She opens the curtains.

You got dressed and then went back to bed? Odd. Oh well, wake up my lady!

She shakes her and quickly realizes that Juliet is not sleeping, but dead.

What the—? No . . . ! NO! HELP! SOMEBODY HELP! My lady is dead! God NO! I wish I'd never been born to see this! Someone get me a drink! MY LORD! MY LADY!

Enter **LADY CAPULET**.

> **LADY CAPULET**: What is going on? Why are you screaming?
>
> **NURSE**: Oh God, what a day!
>
> **LADY CAPULET**: What is the matter?
>
> **NURSE**: Look! Oh, what an awful day!
>
> **LADY CAPULET**: What is—? My daughter—? O my . . . NO! My child?! My life?! No. Wake up. Wake up! Please God, wake up! Open your eyes and look at me or I will die with you. Please . . . please . . . wake up. HELP! Somebody call for help!

Enter **CAPULET**.

> **CAPULET**: This is shameful. What is taking so long? Bring Juliet down. Paris is here!
>
> **NURSE**: She's dead. Deceased. I hate this day. I hate . . .
>
> **LADY CAPULET**: She's dead . . . she's dead! SHE'S DEAD!
>
> **CAPULET**: I don't believe you! Let me see her. What? She's cold. She has no pulse. Her joints are all stiff. She's not breathing . . . it's true. Death is lying on her like a frost on the sweetest flower in the field. She really is . . . dead.
>
> **NURSE**: Horrible day!
>
> **LADY CAPULET**: Horrible morning!
>
> **CAPULET**: I . . . can't . . . speak. I don't have words. It's like death has taken my words just as he took her . . . I can't . . . think.

Enter **FRIAR LAWRENCE, COUNT PARIS,** *and the* **MUSICIANS**.

> **FRIAR LAWRENCE**: Come on everyone! Is the bride ready to go to church?
>
> **CAPULET**: Ready to go, but never to return. *(to Paris)* My son . . . I don't know how to say this. The night before your wedding day, death laid with your

bride. There she is. She belongs to him now. He has taken her. Death is my son-in-law. He is now my heir. I have no other children. I must leave everything to him. My life, my love, her life. All is death's.

PARIS: I've been looking forward to this morning for so long, and this is how it greets me? With this sight?

LADY CAPULET: Accursed, wretched, hateful day! Most miserable hour that time ever saw! I had this one poor and loving child! One child to love and watch grow! One child to see become a woman! One child to take joy in! One child to look on with pride and love! One child . . . and now she's . . . gone. Death stole her from me!

NURSE: Oh God, what a horrible, horrible, terrible, awful day. What a miserable, hateful, wretched day! This is the worst day ever! Nothing could be worse than this! What a day!

PARIS: I've been cheated, divorced, wronged, killed! Death! You have cheated me! You are cruel! You are a monster! Oh love! Oh life! My love is dead!

CAPULET: Despised, distressed, hated, martyred, killed! Why today? Why now? Why would death choose this moment to kill our joy and happiness? Death has not just killed my child, but my soul too. My child is dead, and with my child my joys are buried as well.

FRIAR LAWRENCE: Peace! Stop all this crying and wailing! Shame on you! All of this will not help or solve anything! Listen to me. She was not only your child. She was also a child of God. You were simply sharing her for a time. Well, now she is with God full-time and that is better for her! You could not keep her from death. We all die eventually. But Heaven keeps her soul for eternity. Lord Capulet, you have always said that your ultimate goal was for her advancement and promotion in the world. That is why you agreed to marry her to Paris. And now you are crying? Don't you realize that she just gained the highest advancement and promotion she could ever hope for? She has advanced beyond the clouds as high as Heaven itself! Do you hate your child so much that you go mad seeing her in God's graces? Dying young is not bad; it can be seen as a good thing! Now dry your tears. Stick the rosemary on this beautiful body and, in her finest clothes, carry her to church. Though our human nature tells us to be sad, let us understand that when we use reason, we see she is in eternal joy in high Heaven with the Lord and Father.

CAPULET: Take everything we prepared for the wedding and rework it for a funeral. Our instruments will now be melancholy bells. The wedding feast will now be a burial feast. Our lively music will now be changed to sullen funeral songs. Bridal flowers will now serve for the burial. Take all our joyful decorations and make them mournful.

FRIAR LAWRENCE: Sir, you go ahead, and Madam, you go with him. You too, Count Paris. Everyone prepare to follow this fair body to her grave. The heavens do frown upon you for some unknown offense and it would be bad to do anything that might anger them more.

All but NURSE *and the* MUSICIANS *exit.*

FIRST MUSICIAN: I think it's best if we packed up and left.

NURSE: Yes. That is a good idea. You know this is not a good day.

FIRST MUSICIAN: Absolutely. This day could definitely be better.

NURSE *exits.*

Enter PETER.[91]

PETER: Hey musicians! Don't leave yet! You have to play the song "Heart's Ease!" Please play that song for me!

FIRST MUSICIAN: Why "Heart's Ease?"

PETER: Because I've got a line stuck in my head! My heart is full . . . please play this happy, sad song to comfort me!

FIRST MUSICIAN: No. It's not a good time right now.

PETER: So, you won't play it then?

FIRST MUSICIAN: No.

PETER: Then I will give it to you!

FIRST MUSICIAN: Give us what?

PETER: Not money! That's for dang sure! I will give you an insult! I will call you . . . a minstrel![92]

FIRST MUSICIAN: Okay. Then I'll call you a serving "creature."[93]

---

91   This following exchange between Peter and the musicians is odd. It is almost always cut out of any production, film or stage. My best guess is that Shakespeare used it as a bit of comic relief after such an emotionally taxing scene surrounding Juliet's "death." Basically, we see Peter, who we know is an idiot, trying to request a song of the departing musicians. Most directors don't want to give their audiences this relief and prefer to cut straight to act 5 and keep the emotions riding high as we move to the final act. But it is in the script, so here is the exchange as I interpret it.

92   Oooo!

93   Dang!

PETER: Oh! Then I'll use my dagger on your head! I don't have to take this! I'll take you out! You understand me?

FIRST MUSICIAN: Sure. Fine. Gotcha.

SECOND MUSICIAN: Put the dagger away man. There's no need for that. Just use your words and wit, okay?

PETER: Okay. Fine. You'll regret that! I have the quickest wit ever! You need to answer me like men!

(singing)

When griping griefs the heart doth wound
And doleful dumps the mind oppress,
Then Music with her silver sound—

(talking to the musicians)

Why silver sound? Why music with her silver sound? What do you think, sir?

FIRST MUSICIAN: Because silver has a sweet sound.

PETER: That's stupid. *(to Second Musician)* What do you say?

SECOND MUSICIAN: Umm. Because musicians play for silver coins?

PETER: That's dumb too. *(to Third Musician)* And what do you think?

THIRD MUSICIAN: I have no idea. Enlighten us.

PETER: Oh, you don't know? You all give up? I'll tell you: it is "music with her silver sound" because musicians can't get any gold . . . because they are musicians! Ha! You're poor!

(singing)

Then music with her silver sound
With speedy help doth lend redress.

PETER *exits.*

FIRST MUSICIAN: Wow. What a butt.

SECOND MUSICIAN: Forget him, Jack. Come on. We'll hang out here for awhile and wait for the mourners and then stay for dinner.

They exit.

END OF ACT 4

ACT 5

ACT 5, SCENE 1

Enter ROMEO.

ROMEO: If I can believe in the truth of dreams, then some good news is coming! I dreamed that my lady came to me and found me dead. (Strange that I had the ability to think while dead!) And she brought me back to life with her kisses. I revived and became an emperor! How sweet is love that even just a dream of Juliet can lift my spirits. Today is gonna be a good day!

Enter BALTHASAR, *Romeo's servant, wearing riding boots.*

News from Verona! How are you, Balthasar? Did you bring me any letters from the friar? How is my lady? Is my father well? How is Juliet? I ask that again, because nothing can be bad if she is well!

BALTHASAR: Then she is well and nothing can be bad. Her body sleeps in the Capulet tomb and her soul is with the angels in heaven. I saw them place her dead body in the tomb and then immediately came here to tell you. Forgive me for bringing this horrible news, but it is the job you gave me before you left. I'm so sorry.

ROMEO: What? Are you serious? No. No! I defy you, fate! This is not how this goes! Balthasar, you know where I am staying. Go there and get me some ink and some paper, and then borrow some horses from the inn. I'm going to Verona tonight.

BALTHASAR: I'm begging you sir, be patient and in control. You have that wild look in your eye and I don't trust it. I have this feeling that you are going to do something ... uh ... regretful.

ROMEO: Whatever. I'm fine. Believe me. Now go and do what I ask. Wait. Do you have any letters from the friar?

BALTHASAR: No, my good lord.[94]

ROMEO: Fine. Whatever. Go and make sure to get the horses. I'll catch up.

BALTHASAR *exits.*

Well Juliet, I will lie down with you tonight and then every night for the rest of eternity. Now I just need to find a way to kill myself. Oh Mischief ... you

---

94   This is Shakespeare's way of making sure that the audience understands that Romeo has no idea about the "plan" and is acting on his own.

are quick to enter the thoughts of a desperate man! I remember an apothecary who lives around here. He was an awful, poor, haggard-looking man. Misery had worn him down to the bone! I saw him in his nasty shop. Man, that shop was disgusting. He had tortoises hanging up and a stuffed alligator and other animal skins and weird-looking fish on his shelves. Empty boxes, string, broken pots, and old seeds were everywhere. Seeing all this, I remember thinking, "Wow, if I ever wanted to buy poison, which is illegal and punishable by death in Mantua, this is the dude I would go to to get it." Crazy how I was thinking that before I even needed it. This should be the house and shop. It's closed. Huh, must be a holiday or something. *(yelling)* Hey Apothecary! Are you here? Apothecary!

Enter APOTHECARY.

APOTHECARY: Stop all that yelling. What do you want?

ROMEO: Come here old man. I see that you are poor.[95] *(He offers money.)* Here are forty pieces of gold. Give me some poison that is strong enough to kill a man quickly, straight up.

APOTHECARY: I have drugs like that, but it is against the law for me to sell them. It is punishable by death!

ROMEO: Really?! Look at yourself! Are you really afraid to die?! You look sick! Your life is wretched! I can see the need and oppression in your eyes! Poverty is on your back! Nobody likes you! The world is not your friend and neither are its laws. This corrupt world makes laws that will never allow you to be rich, and you know it. So break the law and stop being poor. Take this money and give me what I ask for.[96]

APOTHECARY: I want to disagree with you. My will and moral code want to say no. But my poverty forces me to say yes.

ROMEO: Then I pay your poverty and not your will. I don't really care what part of you takes the money. I just need the poison.

APOTHECARY: *(giving him the poison)* Put this in any liquid and then drink it all. Then, even if you have the strength of twenty men, you will be dead in minutes.

---

95   Nice.

96   This is an interesting strategy from Romeo. There are a number of ways he could have gone about trying to convince the apothecary to give him poison. He could have lied any number of ways or even appealed to him with the truth of his desire to be with his love for eternity. Instead, he goes on an insult-ridden rant about how the guy's life sucks, but as you see here, it works. Interesting strategy that Shakespeare has Romeo utilize to say the least!

ROMEO: *(handing him the money)* Here is your gold, worse poison to men's souls and responsible for more murders in this loathsome world than this liquid that you can't sell. I sell you the real poison. You haven't sold me any.[97] Farewell, old man. Go buy yourself some food and get some meat on your bones!

APOTHECARY *exits.*

Time to go, my drink. Come with me to Juliet's grave. There is where I must use you.

ROMEO *exits.*

ACT 5, SCENE 2

Enter FRIAR JOHN.

FRIAR JOHN: My brother, Friar Lawrence! Are you here?

Enter FRIAR LAWRENCE.

FRIAR LAWRENCE: That's the voice of Friar John! Welcome back from Mantua! What did Romeo say after reading my letter? Or did he write me back? Give me his letter if he did!

FRIAR JOHN: Yeah . . . about that. Um . . . you see, what had happened was . . . well, I didn't want to walk all the way to Mantua by myself. So I went to find another friar to come with me. He was out visiting and praying over the sick. I found him in a house with some sick people, and while we were there, the town officials declared that house was filled with the plague and they sealed up the doors and windows and wouldn't let us leave. We were quarantined so I couldn't leave the house. I never actually got to Mantua . . . at all . . . sorry.

FRIAR LAWRENCE: Okay, well if you didn't go to Mantua, then who brought my letter to Romeo?

FRIAR JOHN: Nobody. Everyone is so scared of the plague, I couldn't get anybody to even touch it, much less carry it to Mantua. Here it is. *(handing the letter to Friar Lawrence)*[98]

FRIAR LAWRENCE: No, no, no! This is not good! This letter wasn't just a

---

97   I always thought these lines were odd. Romeo is dramatic for sure, but always in matters of love. Romeo comes from a very wealthy family and has never shown any disdain or hatred toward money to this point. These lines don't really seem to fit with his character or anything he has spoken about in the past. I just find them odd. Oh well. Onward!

98   And now we know why Romeo never got the letter!

nice "how are you?" letter! It was full of important information, and Romeo not getting it could cause a lot of trouble! Friar John, go and get a crowbar and bring it to me here. Quickly!

FRIAR JOHN: My brother, I will.

FRIAR JOHN *exits.*

FRIAR LAWRENCE: I have to go to the Capulet tomb myself. Juliet will be waking up in the next three hours. Oh, she is going to be mad when Romeo isn't there. But she can't wake up alone. I'll write another letter to Mantua later and keep her in my room until Romeo can get here. Poor girl, closed up in a dead man's tomb!

He exits.

ACT 5, SCENE 3

Enter **PARIS** *and his* **PAGE**.

PARIS: Give me the torch, boy. Actually, just snuff out the torch. I don't want anyone to see me here. Now, go and lie down underneath those trees over there. Listen carefully and keep an eye out for anybody who may show up in this churchyard, whether they are workers or grave robbers or whatever. If you hear or see anybody, give me a whistle as a signal that someone is here. Give me those flowers. Do as I say. Now, go.

PAGE: *(aside, as he is walking away)* I would really rather not stand around here . . . by myself . . . in a graveyard . . . at night. But a page has to do what a page has to do.

PAGE *moves away from* **PARIS**.

PARIS: *(scattering flowers)* Oh my sweet flower, I will spread these flower petals all over your bridal bed. *(begins to cry)* I will water these flowers every night with my tears! These are the funeral rites I will keep for you, my would-be wife. I will cry for you at your grave!

PAGE *whistles.*

Seriously?! Now?! The boy gives the signal that someone is coming! Who the hell could be here tonight to disturb my own personal ceremony?! And he carries a torch? I'll hide in the darkness and see what he wants.

PARIS *steps aside.*

Enter **ROMEO** *and* **BALTHASAR**.

ROMEO: Give me the mattock and crowbar. Here take this letter. Tomorrow morning, I need you to bring it to my father. Give me the light. Now, I need you to listen to me. On your life, no matter what you see or hear, I need you to stay away and not interrupt me. I need to get into that tomb for a couple reasons. First is to see Juliet's face one more time. But the main reason is that she has a precious ring on her dead finger that I need. It's really important that I get that ring. You understand? So, I need you to leave. But if you do come back to see what I'm doing, by God in Heaven, I will rip off all your limbs and throw them all over this churchyard. I'm going savage here! Do you understand me?

BALTHASAR: I will leave you alone, sir. You'll get no trouble from me.

ROMEO: Then you are a true friend. Take this. *(gives money)* Live and be prosperous. Goodbye, my friend.

BALTHASAR: *(aside as he is walking away)* I don't care what he says. I'm going to hide over here and watch. He has that crazy look in his eye, and I think he is going to do something stupid.

BALTHASAR *hides somewhere on stage.*

ROMEO: *(beginning to force open the tomb)*[99] Disgusting mouth to an awful stomach, you womb of death! You hold the dearest morsel of food this earth has ever seen. I will open these jaws of death and give you even more food to fill your belly!

PARIS: Wait . . . I know him! That is the banished Montague boy who murdered my love's cousin! It was the grief over his death that caused her death! Now he's back to do something villainous to the bodies? Aww, hell no!

(stepping forward)

Stop what you're doing right now, vile Montague! Do you really need to pursue vengeance even beyond death? I am calling for citizen's arrest! You can't be here, so come with me. You must die!

ROMEO: You're absolutely right. I must die. That's why I am here. Good gentleman, I am a desperate man. Don't push me. Please leave me alone. Just go. I'm begging you, don't put another sin on my head by forcing me to hurt or kill you, because if you get in my way, I will do what I have to do. Please be gone. I swear to God I love you more than I love myself right now. I am armed, but I only planned to use my weapon on myself—no one else. Leave and live. Just say that a madman's mercy asked you to leave!

---

99   Alright . . . metaphor time!

PARIS: Oh, shut up! I don't believe a word you say! Now come with me, you criminal!

ROMEO: Really? Now you provoke me? Fine. Have it your way. Bring it on boy!

They draw their swords and begin to fight.

PAGE: Oh man! They're fighting! I'll go get the watch!

PAGE *exits.*[100]

PARIS: Oh! God! I'm hit. I'm dying! The blood . . . what . . . why . . . God. *(He coughs a few times and spits some blood.)* If you have any mercy in your soul, please open the tomb and place my body next to Juliet.

PARIS *dies.*[101]

ROMEO: In faith, I will. Let me see who this guy was . . . Mercutio's cousin, the noble Count Paris?! Holy crap! Wait . . . what did Balthasar say when we were riding here? Dangit, I wasn't paying attention! I think he was saying something about how Paris was supposed to marry Juliet. Was that it? Or did I dream that? Or am I just going crazy thinking about Juliet? Huh. Oh well. Give me your hand and you can join me in misfortune. I'll bury you in this glorious grave.

---

[100]   The fight continues. It is competitive with Paris being a trained fighter, but he cannot match the violence, aggressiveness, and passion of Romeo. It rages for a bit, but Paris does not want to kill anyone. He only wants to subdue Romeo for arrest. Whereas Romeo is like a cornered animal with nothing to lose; he ultimately gets a mortal strike in against Paris.

[101]   This scene is often cut out of movies and productions of this play. This is a fight scene culminating in the death of one of the major characters. Why is this scene so often cut? I think it is the same reason that a lot of Romeo's lines are cut down in the early scenes. Directors want to keep the idea that Romeo is the ideal romantic lead. And the fact is, as Shakespeare wrote him, he is not. Paris may not be all that likeable, but the man did nothing wrong. He went through all of the proper channels for this marriage. Based on this scene alone, he seemed to truly care about Juliet; he did not see her as a trophy or political pawn. In this scene, he is actually trying to protect the bodies of Juliet and her cousin. He has no knowledge of the secret marriage and knows only that the Montagues and Capulets are feuding and Romeo was on the front line of that feud by killing Tybalt. Romeo killing Paris (without actually even knowing who he was) just underscores Romeo as a brash, impulsive, highly immature young man who lets his emotions rule him to the detriment of all logic. This scene would drop his status in the audience's eyes—further proof that he is not the ideal romantic lead. So in order to protect Romeo's image and reputation, this scene is oftentimes left out.

ROMEO *opens the tomb and drags Paris's body inside.*

A grave? No. This is a room of light! For there lies Juliet and she brings light to this dim tomb!

Lays Paris in the tomb.

How often do men actually feel happy near the point of death? Knowing that the trials of life will soon be no more and eternal sleep awaits. That is not the case with me. I can't feel happy right now. Oh my love, my wife, Death has taken your breath, but he has not had any effect on your beauty! Your lips and cheeks are still bright! Weird, I thought you would be pale by now![102] *(to Tybalt)* Tybalt, is that you lying underneath that bloody sheet? What more can I do for you than to kill the man who killed you . . . meaning myself. Forgive me, my cousin. *(to Juliet)* Ah, dear Juliet, why are you still so beautiful?[103] Is death in love with you as well? Does he keep you this way so he can come here in the dark and make love to you? To protect you from that, I will stay here in this dim palace with you for eternity. I will never leave you again. Here with the worms I will set up my everlasting rest. Eyes, take your last look. Arms, take your last embrace. *(hugs Juliet)* And lips, with a righteous kiss you will seal a contract with death for all time.

Kisses Juliet.

I am the desperate pilot of my sinking ship, which is now crashing on the sharp rocks of fate. I am weary of the seasickness I feel in this life. Here's to my love! *(drinking)* Oh true apothecary, you didn't lie! Your drugs work fast! Thus, with a kiss, I die.

ROMEO *dies.*

Enter **FRIAR LAWRENCE** *into the churchyard with a lantern, a crowbar, and a spade shovel.*

FRIAR LAWRENCE: Saint Francis help me! How often tonight have my old feet stumbled over graves! —Who's there?

BALTHASAR: A friend that you know well.

FRIAR LAWRENCE: Bliss be upon you. Tell me, my good friend, why is there a torch burning here in a graveyard? As far as I can tell, it seems to be burning at the Capulet tomb!

BALTHASAR: Yes sir, it is there and it belongs to my master. Someone you love.

---

102   OMG!

103   *OMG!!!*

FRIAR LAWRENCE: Someone . . . I . . . love . . . oh no. Who is it?

BALTHASAR: Romeo.

FRIAR LAWRENCE: Oh my God. How long has he been there?

BALTHASAR: Half an hour or so.

FRIAR LAWRENCE: Oh lord. Come with me to the tomb!

BALTHASAR: Oh, um, sorry, but no. My master thinks I'm gone and basically told me he would brutally murder me if I stuck around. I don't want him to know I'm still here. I'm sure you understand.

FRIAR LAWRENCE: Fine. Stay then. I'll go alone. I've got a really bad feeling about this. I'm afraid something terrible has happened.

BALTHASAR: Oh hey, there's one more thing. I was kinda dozing over here, so it may have just been a dream, but I think my master may have fought another guy and killed him. I may have dreamed it, but just in case . . . you know, FYI.

FRIAR LAWRENCE *looks at Balthasar with no words to say and begins to move toward the tomb.*

FRIAR LAWRENCE: Romeo! Romeo! Are you . . . here? Why is there blood all over the entrance of the tomb? And why are there bloody swords on the ground in front of this place of peace? Oh God. This is not good.

FRIAR LAWRENCE *enters the tomb.*

Romeo! Oh no, he's pale! He's dead?! Wait, who else is here? Paris?! Covered in blood? He's dead as well?! Oh my lord, this is a terrible night! A terrible hour!

JULIET *starts to wake up.*

The lady stirs.

JULIET: Friar? Friar! I'm so happy to see you! Where is my lord? I remember where I am and everything that was supposed to happen. Romeo is supposed to be here. Where is he? Where is my Romeo?

FRIAR LAWRENCE: I hear some noises and I'm freaking out here! Lady, come, get off of that slab of death. A greater power than we can control, fate, has messed up our plans. Come on, let's get out of here. Your husband is right here and he is dead. And Paris is over there and he is dead too. Come on, let's get out of this place. I'll put you into a sisterhood of holy nuns. Don't just stand there and ask questions, just move! The watch are on their way! Come on! We can't stay here any longer!

JULIET: Go on! Get out of here! I'm not leaving!

FRIAR LAWRENCE *exits.*[104]

What is this? A cup closed in my true love's hand? Poison. That's what he used. Poison. And you drank it all? You couldn't leave even a drop for me to use? I will kiss your lips. Maybe there is some left there for me so that I may also die. *(She kisses him.)* Your lips are still warm!

Enter Paris's PAGE *and* THE WATCH *into the churchyard.*

FIRST WATCH: Lead the way, boy. Which way?

JULIET: I hear something. Then I'll make this quick. I see Romeo's dagger. My body will be your sheath from now on. There you may rust and let me die.

She takes Romeo's dagger, stabs herself, and dies.

PAGE: This is the place, there where the torch is burning.

FIRST WATCH: The ground is bloody—search the area. You men, anybody you find in the area, arrest on suspicion and bring them to me.

Some watchmen exit. FIRST WATCH *and others enter the tomb.*

Oh what a terrible sight. Count Paris is dead and Juliet is bleeding . . . and warm. She seems to be dead . . . again . . . after being buried for two days? Somebody go tell the prince! Then go wake the Capulets and the Montagues. The rest of you, go search the area. Let's get to the bottom of this.

Others exit.

Enter WATCHMEN *with Romeo's man,* BALTHASAR.

SECOND WATCH: Here's Romeo's man. We found him in the churchyard.

FIRST WATCH: Hold onto him until the prince gets here.

Enter WATCHMEN *with* FRIAR LAWRENCE.

THIRD WATCH: Here is a friar that trembles, sighs, and weeps. We took this mattock and spade from him as he was leaving the churchyard.

---

104   I've always wondered about this. He doesn't even put up a fight! He doesn't argue with her or try to reason with her—as he always tried to do with Romeo. He doesn't try to remove her or anything. For a character who is one of those most responsible for this mess, he runs away and abandons a thirteen-year-old girl quite quickly!

FIRST WATCH: Hmm . . . very suspicious. Hold him too.

Enter PRINCE *and* ATTENDANTS.

PRINCE: What is so important that I had to get out of bed so early?

Enter CAPULET *and* LADY CAPULET.

CAPULET: What is going on? Why is everybody yelling?

LADY CAPULET: People in the streets are crying out "Romeo" while others are crying out "Juliet," and still others scream the name of Paris. And everybody is running to our tomb. What is this?

PRINCE: Somebody explain.

FIRST WATCH: Your Highness, here lies Count Paris. He's been killed. Here is Romeo, also dead, and finally, Juliet, who was dead before, seems to have warmed back to life but now is dead again.

PRINCE: Somebody better know how all of this happened and speak up!

FIRST WATCH: Well, we do have Romeo's servant and this friar who had the proper tools to open a tomb.

CAPULET: Oh heavens! Oh wife! Look how our daughter bleeds! The dagger from that Montague is sheathed in our daughter's chest! Oh God!

LADY CAPULET: This sight will be the death of me! I can't handle this!

Enter MONTAGUE.

PRINCE: Come Montague, you are up too early to see your son and heir so early down.

MONTAGUE: Alas, my liege, my wife is dead tonight. The grief of her only son's exile has stopped her breath. What could possibly happen to make this day any worse?

PRINCE: Look and you will see.

MONTAGUE: *(seeing Romeo dead)* What?! No! Why God, why? This is too much! This will send me to my own grave! I can't . . . I just can't . . . do . . . this . . . why?

PRINCE: Right now, I need everybody to remain calm. I can't have fingers being pointed and outrage ruling the day. We need to find out how this happened. We need to hear the details and the causes of this tragedy. Once we know the whole story, then trust me, I will lead you in our mourning. We have all felt loss. But until then, we need patience. Bring forth those men of suspicion.

FRIAR LAWRENCE: I can explain much of this. I am of the greatest suspicion in this terrible murder. So I stand here ready to condemn myself but also to free myself from the weight of the secrets I carry.

PRINCE: Tell us what you know.

FRIAR LAWRENCE: I will try to keep this short. Romeo, there dead, was the husband to Juliet, and she was his faithful wife. I married them, and their wedding day was also the same day as Tybalt's death, whose untimely demise resulted in the banishment of the newly married Romeo. It was for him, not Tybalt, that Juliet grieved. You, Lord Capulet, in order to cure her grief, decided to force her to marry Count Paris. She then came to me, wild-eyed and suicidal, to try and get out of this second marriage. Otherwise, she would have killed herself right there in my church. So we came up with a plan. I gave her a potion—because I am an expert in herbal medicines and their properties—that would put her in a deep sleep that mimicked death in every way. In the meantime, I wrote a letter to Romeo explaining the plan and that he should be here at this hour when she was to wake up so he could run away with her. But unfortunately, the man who was supposed to carry the letter, Friar John, was quarantined by accident and returned my letter to me. So I came to this tomb by myself with the intention of hiding her in my room at the church until I could send a new letter to Romeo. But when I got here, just a few minutes before she woke up, I found the dead bodies of both Paris and Romeo already lying on the ground. She woke up and I begged her to be patient and come away with me, but then some noise scared me from the tomb. She would not go with me but did some violence unto herself instead. This is everything I know. Her nurse also knows about the marriage and can attest to that. If you find that this is all my fault, I will not deny it or fight it. I will sacrifice my old life to the severest punishment according to law.

PRINCE: We still believe you to be a holy man, Friar. Thank you for the information. Where is Romeo's man? What does he have to say?

BALTHASAR: I saw the funeral, so I went to Mantua and told Romeo about Juliet's death. Then we immediately rented some horses and came straight to this tomb. He gave me this letter with the instructions to deliver it to his father in the morning. And then he threatened to kill me if I didn't leave the churchyard.

PRINCE: Give me the letter. I'll take a look at it.

He takes Romeo's letter.

Where is the count's page who came and got the watch? Why was your master here tonight?

PAGE: He came with flowers to cover his lady's grave. He told me to go hide and I did. Then some people came with a torch to open the tomb and, after some words, my master drew his sword and they started fighting. That's when I left to get the watch.

PRINCE: This letter verifies everything the friar said. It describes his love for Juliet and how he heard of her death. He writes that he bought poison from a poor apothecary and then came to this tomb to die and lie with Juliet. —Where are these enemies? Capulet and Montague, do you see the ramifications of your hate? Heaven found a way to kill your joys with love! And I, for allowing this feud to continue, have lost two cousins! Everyone is punished!

CAPULET: O brother Montague, give me your hand. This is my daughter's wedding present. The end of our fight is all I can ask for.

MONTAGUE: I will give you more. I will raise a statue of Juliet in pure gold. That way, for as long as Verona stands, no one will ever be held in as high regard as that of true and faithful Juliet.

CAPULET: And I will raise a statue of Romeo, also in pure gold, to lie by his lady for all time. These are the sacrifices we must make for our hatred.

PRINCE: This morning brings with it a glooming peace.
It remains dark; the sun won't show his head.
Talk of sadness and how hatred will cease.
Some shall be pardoned, and some punish-ed.
For never was a story of more woe
Than this of Juliet and her Romeo.

All exit.

END OF ACT 5

FURTHER READING

For those looking for some additional material to read, look no further than the actual text of *Romeo and Juliet* by the one and only William Shakespeare. Now that you have read this version, you know the plot, the characters, the drama, and everything else. Now it is time to read the original and enjoy it for the beautiful language of Shakespeare. I believe you will enjoy it that much more!

The edition I have always preferred to read is from the Folger Shakespeare Library and their Shakespeare Set Free series. It has some wonderful background material on Shakespeare's life and theatre, and their definitions and explanations of the text are very well organized and helpful. That being said, since the work is in the public domain, the full text is available anywhere, throughout the web, for your reading pleasure.

For complete texts of all of Shakespeare's works, as well as a concordance, statistics, and all sorts of other fun info, you can visit Open Source Shakespeare. It has a wealth of knowledge! You can find more information here: https://www.opensourceshakespeare.org.

If you do have the itch to read the original Shakespeare texts, you will most likely come across words and phrases that are unfamiliar to you. Have no fear! There are a number of Shakespeare glossary websites, specifically catered to the Bard, that will have all those phrases and words that are no longer used in today's English. Check them out:

> https://www.shakespeareswords.com/Public/Glossary.aspx
> https://www.nosweatshakespeare.com/dictionary/
> http://www.shakespeare-online.com/glossary/

Also, if you want to add some acting-specific nuance to your work, you can check out *Will Power: How to Act Shakespeare in 21 Days* by John Basil with Stephanie Gunning. It gives some wonderful tips and drills to help students become better actors when performing Shakespeare's plays (although most of the advice can be used in any acting capacity!).

Finally, if you are in the mood for analysis, literary criticism, and reviews of Shakespeare's works, you can check out the databases and e-books provided by Gale. You can find more information here: https://www.gale.com/shakespearean-criticism.

ACKNOWLEDGMENTS

The publication of this book was partially supported by crowdfunding. I would like to take a moment to acknowledge my wonderful and generous family members, friends, acquaintances, colleagues, classmates, former students, and complete strangers who contributed to this little project.

Thanks go to Brittni Parrish, Kaia Hirt, Cari Brastad, Pete Evans, Lisa DeLaHunt, Jan Scearcy, Warren Salvog, Hannah Ungerman, Amie Weaver, Lisa Jones, Erin Thein, Abbi Dion, Kristin A. Miner, Sonja Leaf, Kristen Mueller, Sandra Brown, Lori Stroner, Bob Wichmann, Aileen Devitt White, Eleanor Stoltz, Holy Guncheon, Kirsten Bighia, Grace Singer, Cindy Reents, Bridget Simpson, Dan Paulson, Tori and Jerad Newman, Lesley Stoesz, Julia Lutz, Alexandra Rymer, Dana Menard, Lisa Horner, Peter Schultz, William Schultz, Paradise Schultz, Tom Mayer, Vicki Poels, Elizabeth Nuytten, Anna Schultz, Jacob Haarstad, Samuel Boggs, Michelle Varholdt, Nikki Manson, Jackie Edgett, Sharon Heiman, Mary Jo Peterson, Don and Mary Bakke, Kirsten Griebenow, Melissa Schuchmann, Anne Beaton, Mark Chergosky, Bonnie Hansen, Dawn DeLude, Jessica Berg, Renee Gallup, Karen Griffiths, Krissy Dieruf, Debbie Grossman, James Taylor Anderson, Tyler and Melissa Lam, Carin Call, Janet Lane, Luis Lopez, Linnea Haley, James Peterson, Patty W., and Jenny Tousignant.

I, of course, want to thank my family. I could not have done this without you. To my wife, Kirsten Griebenow; my daughter, MacKenna Bakke; my parents, Don and Mary Bakke; my brother, Josh Bakke, and his family; and my in-laws, Kim and Sharlene Griebenow, I give my heartfelt thanks. Words aren't enough. I would like to name all of my family for their support throughout my life, but there simply isn't room! You know who you are!

I would also like to thank the wonderful people at Theran Press, and Dr. Peter Schultz in particular, for their immense support, feedback, and encouragement. This was a process that began years ago and their support never wavered. For that, I am forever grateful.

I would like to thank my many colleagues in the English Department of Robbinsdale Armstrong High School who encouraged me to finish what began as a little one-and-done lesson plan to get from point A to point B in our Romeo and Juliet unit. Their willingness to try it, give feedback, and bring it into their classrooms has been incredible. Many shared my crowdfunding page and many donated to help make this happen. I am forever grateful to Kirsten Bighia, Robert Maas, Kaia Hirt, Brittni Parrish, Abbi Dion, Morgan McCann, and Linnea Haley for sharing in its growth, as well as Anne Beaton, Jenny Lovitt, Jodi Maxymek, Linnea Fischer, Stacy Olstadt, Melissa Schuchmann, Darren Heydanek, Brent Olson, Kevin Martinson, Jacob Vyskocil, Leigh Hendrickson, Katie Fuller, Faye Rylander, Cathryn Peterson, Lee Fisher, Erin Sinner, Travis Kern, Aaron Kesher, Erin Thein, and Michael Hasapopoulos for supporting me throughout the years and showing me how to be a teacher. I'm not who I am without you.

Finally, I would like to thank my students, both current and former. The truth is that this doesn't exist without you. I don't write this without you. It goes without saying that this is for you and for all the future students who come into contact with this book. Some former students are listed above as donors who supported the publication of this project. Luis, James, Alexandra, Julia, and Grace, you are amazing.

And, on a final note: thank you, the reader, for picking this up and giving it a chance. I truly hope you enjoy it and learn a little bit too!

ANTHONY BAKKE (*BS, Communication Arts and Literature, St. Cloud State University; MS, Education and Professional Development, University of Wisconsin–River Falls*) is an English teacher at Robbinsdale Armstrong High School in Plymouth, Minnesota. He has been teaching since 2004. When he is not teaching, he can be found coaching high school baseball, playing men's softball, golfing, drawing, or playing the guitar. He lives in Minneapolis, Minnesota with his wife, Kirsten, and daughter, MacKenna, along with their dog, Neesa.

Made in the USA
Monee, IL
07 February 2024

52600842R00059